RAND McNALLY

HISTORICAL ATLAS OF THE HOLY LAND

Edited by Emil G. Kraeling

RAND McNALLY & COMPANY

New York   CHICAGO   San Francisco

Contents

Contents

Contents

The Land
of the Bible

A DOORWAY from the ruins of Persepolis, guarded on the right by a winged and human-headed bull from Khorsabad in Assyria, fittingly symbolizes the ancient Oriental civilizations. On the left an oracle from a Dead Sea Scroll declares that "peoples labor only for fire" (Hab. 2:13). The ruin-mounds or *tells,* in which lie the remains of hundreds of walled cities that were destroyed by fire, confirm the word of the Lord.

For more than a century archaeologists have been exploring some of these mounds. They have recovered a vast amount of history of which nothing was known to the ancient Greek writers. But Palestine furnished little to whet the public appetite. In April of 1948, however, it came into its own, when the announcement was made that ancient manuscripts of the time of Christ had turned up. They had been found by Arab tribesmen in a cave near the Dead Sea. A dealer from Bethlehem had negotiated their

sale in part to an archbishop at Jerusalem and in part to an archaeologist of the Hebrew University. It was in the midst of the war between Israelis and Arabs over the establishment of the state of Israel.

The cave was in Jordan territory and the Amman Department of Antiquities located it in January, 1949. It was near Khirbet Qumran, an ancient ruined site on a bluff overlooking the northern end of the Dead Sea (*see* 1 and 6). The Department carried on a careful exploration of it, recovering fragments of some seventy different manuscripts in the debris. The archbishop, who had shown his Scrolls to scholars at the American School of Archaeology, brought them to the United States, where all but one were edited. The Scroll to receive the most attention was a great, nearly complete copy of Isaiah, written on leather in the first century B.C., with fifty-four columns of beautiful Hebrew writing.

5

1. **DEAD SEA SCROLLS AREA**

1. The Scrolls' discovery led to a further ransacking of caves by Bedouin and by archaeologists from 1952 on. The original cave (1Q) lies ½ mile north of Wadi Qumran. In 3Q two copper scrolls were discovered. Tremendously important was cave 4Q in the ledge below Khirbet Qumran. It is visible at the bottom left of illustration 6. Cave 11Q, the 1956 Bedouin discovery, produced nearly complete rolls and thus ranks with Caves 1 and 4. In 1952 the Bedouin found manuscripts in caves at the Wadi Murabba'at, 12 miles farther south, but these belonged to the period between A.D. 70 and 135. A letter of the Jewish rebel leader Bar Kochba was among the finds. Manuscripts found hereabouts show that the Old Testament text had been stabilized to its present form by A.D. 135. An important Septuagint Greek text of the Minor Prophets was also found in this vicinity by Bedouin.

2. On the left, above the western shore of the Dead Sea which is 3,000 feet below this vantage point, lies a square patch of land. It is the now excavated Khirbet Qumran (see 6), the home of the Dead Sea Scrolls community. The photograph was taken from Mt. Nebo, and thus also shows Moses' view of the Promised Land. Spread out before the eyes lies the wilderness of Judah. On the high ground, from right to left, a close study reveals the Russian tower on the Mt. of Olives, and something of Jerusalem. A little left of center lies Bethlehem, with the Frank Mountain, on which stood the Herodium (see 48), to the southeast of it. The heights toward Hebron, rich in the memory of the patriarchs, appear farther to the left. To poor Bedouin from the Arabian wastes who saw from afar that green land on the high ground, it truly seemed a land flowing with milk and honey. To seize it was the objective not only of the Israelites but of tribesmen of many ages, as archaeology has shown.

2.   MATSON PHOTO SERVICE

3. Looking out from the inside of the prize cave of them all—4Q, in which were stored over 400 manuscripts, many of them non-Biblical and otherwise unknown. While the archaeologists were following new leads in the Wadi Murabba'at area, leaving Qumran deserted, the Bedouin found this cave in the summer of 1952. They dug out the debris which was over 3 feet deep, and no doubt full of manuscript fragments. Hearing of this, the archaeologists hastened back in time to glean a great number of fragments. It appears that the Qumran residents stored their main library here when the Romans swept down on them in A.D. 68.

4. One of the two copper scrolls representing a single text, found in Cave 3Q. About 12 inches high, they were originally a single roll, 3 feet long, of three riveted sheets. The text is written in the late Hebrew known from the Mishnah, the oldest part of the Talmud. It lists about 60 treasures and their locations, most of which are at Jerusalem or in Judaea. Another copy of the document "with explanations, measurements and all details" is allegedly hidden in a certain pit. Descriptions of the hiding places were only understandable to those familiar with the localities. Thus 600 bars of silver are reported hidden "in the cistern which is below the rampart on the east side, in a place hollowed out of the rock." Tombs, such as that of Zadok (2 Sam. 8:17?) and the cairn of Achan in the valley of Achor (Josh. 7:26) are among the hiding places. The total of treasure is said to amount to 200 tons of gold and silver! A work of the imagination?

5. The Isaiah Scroll from Qumran was unrolled from left to right by its readers. You can see where their hands held it. As Hebrew was written from right to left, the next column was always to the left. The height of the scroll is 22½ inches. The completely visible column covers most of Isaiah 40. It starts with the words in v. 2 "that her warfare is accomplished." Notice the paragraphing and the interlinear or marginal additions. Jesus was handed such a scroll in the synagogue at Nazareth. When he "opened" and "closed" it, he actually unrolled it and rolled it up (Lk. 4:17, 20).

7

6.   PALESTINE ARCHAEOLOGICAL MUSEUM

6. The Qumran ruins, as they appeared from the air after they had been excavated (1951-56). The place was obviously a fortified refuge and communal center. The people may have lived round about in caves, huts, or tents. The aqueduct (16) brought down precious water from Wadi Qumran in the rainy season. The entrance was from the north side (14). The scriptorium, where inkwells and tables were found, suggesting that the Scrolls-copyists labored here, was at 26. Hoards of coins from the 1st century B.C. were found in 18. The council chamber (25) and the assembly and banquet hall (1) with attached pantry (2) command great interest. The kitchen was in 12, a bread oven in 24.

The place was damaged by an earthquake in 31 B.C., and according to the coins seems to have been unoccupied until after the death of Herod in 4 B.C. It was destroyed by the Romans in A.D. 68.

Other features include cisterns (10, 19, 30, 31), laundry (9), bath (17), potters' workshop (4-7), industrial kilns (23), storerooms (20), courtyards (2, 15). Traces of older Israelite settlement on the site are to be found in a cistern (21) and a building corner (8). This may have been the City of Salt of Josh. 15:62.

7. Storage bins in the Qumran settlement, with a channel for water leading by.

7.   PALESTINE ARCHAEOLOGICAL MUSEUM

MAP I

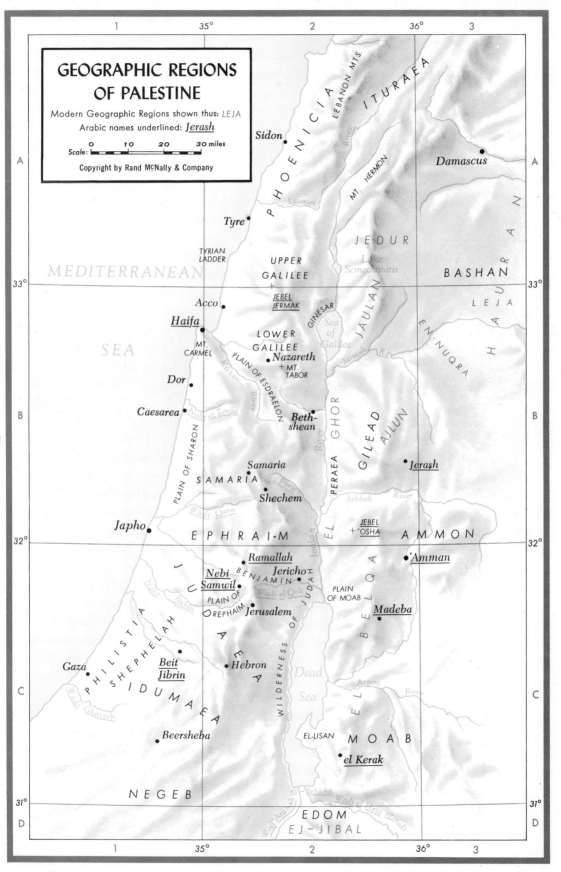

GEOGRAPHIC REGIONS OF PALESTINE

Modern Geographic Regions shown thus: LEJA

Arabic names underlined: *Jerash*

Scale: 0   10   20   30 miles

Copyright by Rand McNally & Company

Sidon

Damascus

Tyre

LEBANON MTS.

ITURAEA

PHOENICIA

MT. HERMON

HAURAN

JEDUR

BASHAN

Leontes

River

Lake
Semechonitis

LEJA

MEDITERRANEAN

TYRIAN
LADDER

Acco

UPPER
GALILEE

JEBEL
JERMAK

GINESAR

Sea
of
Galilee

JAULAN

EN-NUQRA

Haifa

MT.
CARMEL

LOWER
GALILEE

Nazareth

MT.
TABOR

SEA

Dor

PLAIN OF ESDRAELON

Kishon

River

Beth-
shean

GHOR

GILEAD

AJLUN

Caesarea

Nahr ez Zerga

PLAIN OF SHARON

PERAEA

Jerash

Samaria

W. Fara

River

Jabbok

River

Shechem

Wadi Qana

EL

Japho

EPHRAIM

Jordan

JEBEL
OSHA

AMMON

Ramallah

BENJAMIN

Jericho

'Amman

Nebi
Samwil

JUDAH

PLAIN OF

Wadi el Qelt

PLAIN
OF MOAB

Madeba

Nahr

Rubin

REPHAIM

Jerusalem

WILDERNESS OF JUDAH

EL

BELQA

PHILISTIA

SHEPHELAH

JUDAEA

Beit
Jibrin

Hebron

Dead

Sea

Amon

River

Gaza

IDUMAEA

Wadi

Ghazzeh

Beersheba

EL-LISAN

MOAB

el Kerak

NEGEB

es Sebkha

Wadi el Hesa (Zared)

Wadi Araba

EDOM
EJ-JIBAL

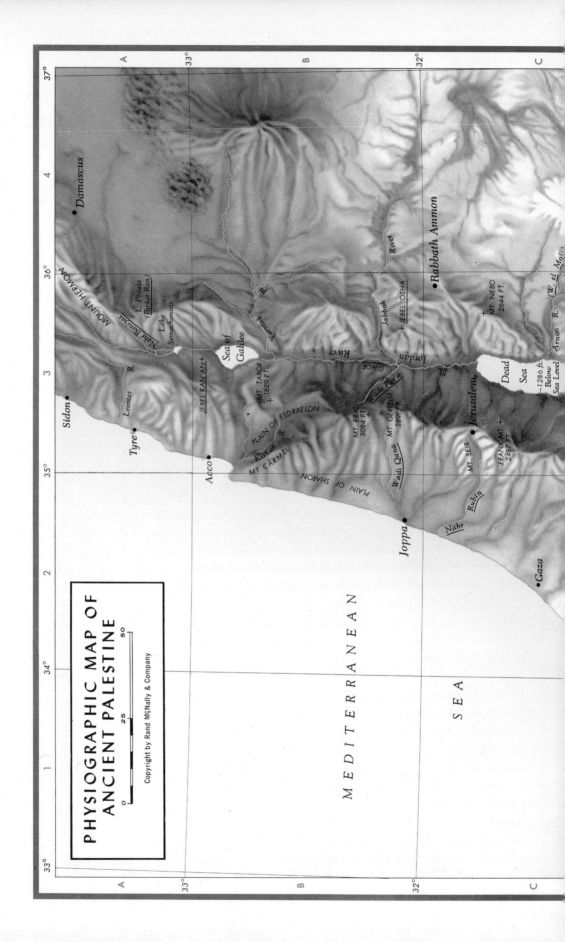

PHYSIOGRAPHIC MAP OF
ANCIENT PALESTINE

Copyright by Rand McNally & Company

0   25   50

MEDITERRANEAN

SEA

Damascus

MOUNT HERMON

Nahr Baniyas

L. Phiala
(Birket Ram)

Lake
Semechonitis

Sidon

Leontes R.

Tyre

JEBEL KAN'AN

Sea of
Galilee

Yarmuk R.

Acco

MT. TABOR
+ 1820 FT.

PLAIN OF ESDRAELON

MT. CARMEL

Kishon R.

PLAIN OF SHARON

Wadi Qana

Joppa

Nahr Rubin

Gaza

MT. EBAL
3084 FT.

MT. GERIZIM
2891 FT.

Wadi Far'a

GHOR

Jordan River

El GHOR

Jabbok

JEBEL 'OSHA

River

Rabbath Ammon

MT. NEBO
+ 2644 FT.

W. el Mojib

Armon R.

MT. SEIR

FRANK MT. +
2487 FT.

Jerusalem

Dead
Sea

−1286 ft.
Below
Sea Level

10

MAP II

SHIHAN

Sebkha Brook of Zered (W. el Hesa)

Wadi el 'Arabah

es

•Ma'an

JEBEL RAMM +
5397 FT.

N E G E B

MOUNT
HALAK

Ezion-
geber •

Gulf
of
Aqabah

N •Kadesh-
barnea

JEBEL KHARÛF +
3395 FT.

JEBEL HELAL +
2926 FT.

JEBEL YELEQ +
3566 FT.

31° D 30° E

31° D 30° E

4

36°

3

35°

2

34°

1

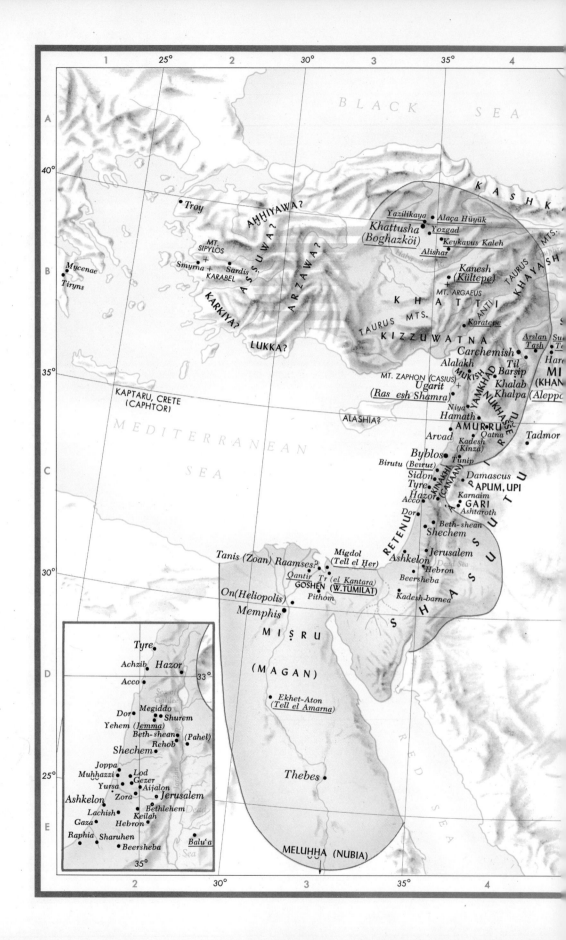

MAP III

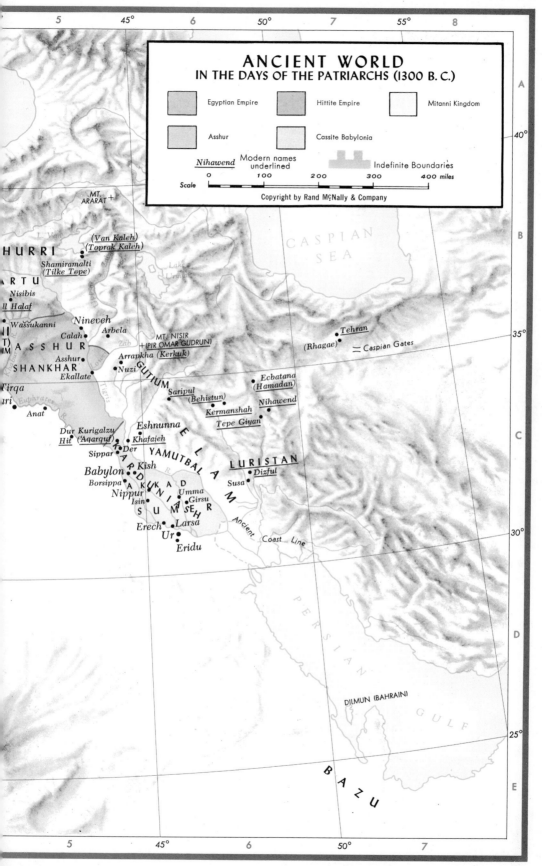

ANCIENT WORLD
IN THE DAYS OF THE PATRIARCHS (1300 B.C.)

Egyptian Empire   Hittite Empire   Mitanni Kingdom

Asshur   Cassite Babylonia

Nihawend Modern names underlined   Indefinite Boundaries

Scale 0 100 200 300 400 miles

Copyright by Rand McNally & Company

MT. ARARAT

HURRI

RTU

(Van Kaleh)
(Toprak Kaleh)

Shamiramalti
(Tilke Tepe)

Nisibis

Il Halaf

Wassukanni

Nineveh

Arbela

CASPIAN SEA

Lake Urmia

Tehran

(Rhagae)   Caspian Gates

MT. NISIR
(PIR OMAR GUDRUN)

ASSHUR

Calah

NT)
IM

SHANKHAR

Asshur

Arrapkha (Kerkuk)

Nuzi

Ekallate

Zab

Tirqa

Anat

Euphrates R.

Saripul
(Behistun)

Ecbatana
(Hamadan)

Kermanshah

Nihawend

Tepe Giyan

Eshnunna

Dur Kurigalzu
('Aqarquf)

Hit

Khafajeh

Der

Sippar

Babylon

Borsippa

Nippur

Isin

Kish

KARDUNIASH

YAMUTBAL

AKKAD

SUMER

Umma

Girsu

SEH

Erech

Larsa

Ur

Eridu

ELAM

LURISTAN

Dizful

Susa

Ancient Coast Line

Tigris

PERSIAN GULF

DILMUN (BAHRAIN)

BAZU

5   45°   6   50°   7

13

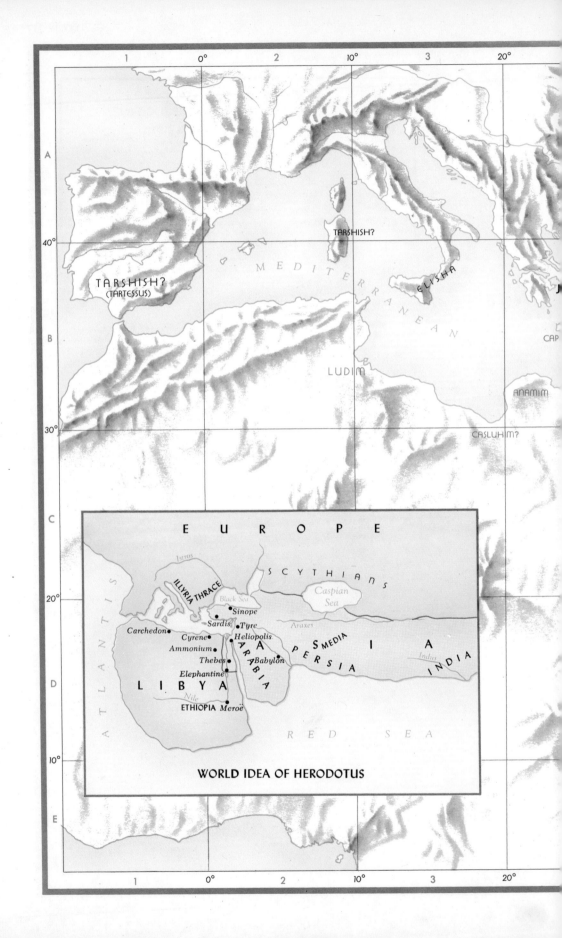

TARSHISH?

TARSHISH?
(TARTESSUS)

ELISHA

M E D I T E R R A N E A N

LUDIM

CAP

ANAMIM

CASLUHIM?

E U R O P E

Istros

ILLYRIA THRACE

S C Y T H I A N S

Caspian
Sea

ATLANTIS

Black Sea

•Sinope

Sardis• •Tyre

Carchedon•

•Cyrene •Heliopolis

Ammonium•

A

Axares

S MEDIA I A

A R A B I A

Indus

P E R S I A

INDIA

Thebes• •Babylon

Elephantine•

L I B Y A

Nile

ETHIOPIA Meroë•

R E D   S E A

WORLD IDEA OF HERODOTUS

MAP IV

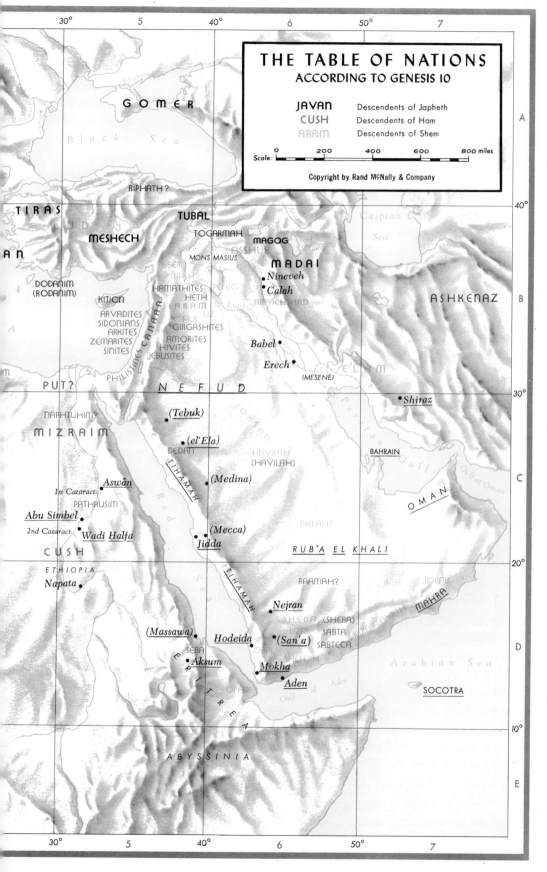

THE TABLE OF NATIONS
ACCORDING TO GENESIS 10

JAVAN   Descendents of Japheth
CUSH   Descendents of Ham
ARAM   Descendents of Shem

Scale: 0   200   400   600   800 miles

Copyright by Rand McNally & Company

GOMER

Black   Sea

RIPHATH?

TIRAS

TUBAL

MESHECH

TOGARMAH

MAGOG

MONS MASIUS

MADAI

ASSHUR

•Nineveh
•Calah

DODANIM
(RODANIM)

KITION

HAMATHITES
HETH
ARAM

PELEG

ARPACHSHAD

ASHKENAZ

ARVADITES
SIDONIANS
ARKITES
ZEMARITES
SINITES

HUL
GIRGASHITES
AMORITES
HIVITES
JEBUSITES

UZ

Babel•

Erech•

ELAM

A

PUT?

PHILISTINES

CANAAN

N E F U D

(MESENE)

•Shiraz

NAPHTUHIM?

MIZRAIM

(Tebuk)•

•(el'Ela)
DEDAN

HAVILAH
(HAVILAH)

BAHRAIN

Caspian
Sea

Gulf of Oman

1st Cataract
Aswân

PATHRUSIM

TIHAMAH

(Medina)•

O M A N

Abu Simbel
2nd Cataract Wadi Halfa•

•(Mecca)
Jidda•

DIKLAH?

RUB'A EL KHALI

JOKTAN

Red

Gulf

CUSH

ETHIOPIA
Napata•

RAAMAH?

JORAB

MAHRA

(Massawa)•

Hodeida•

Nejran•

SHEBA (SHEBA)

SABTA
•(San'a) SABTECA

SEBA
•Aksum

Mokha•

•Aden

Arabian Sea.

SOCOTRA

OPHIR

ERITREA

Gulf of Aden

A B Y S S I N I A

Blue Nile

15

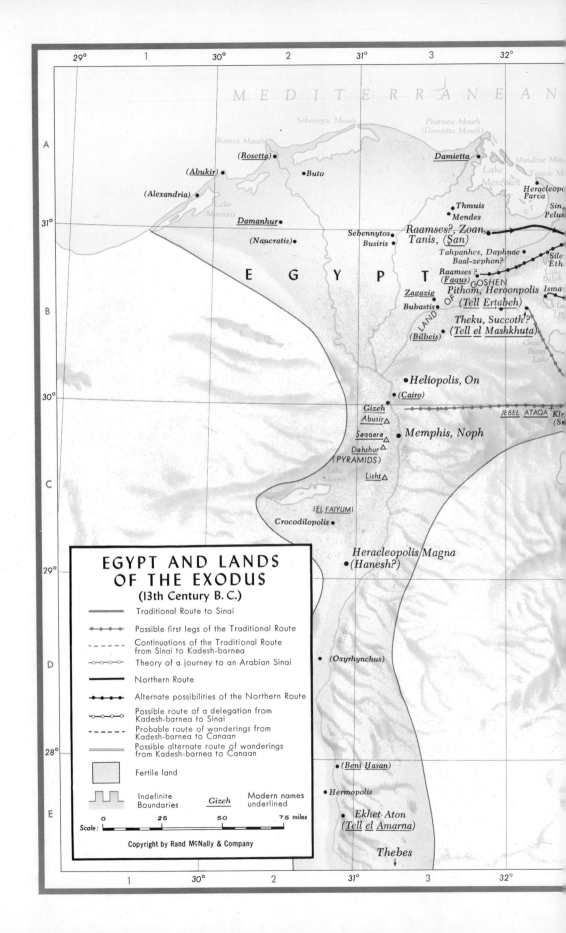

MEDITERRANEAN

A

Sebennytic Mouth
Rosetta Mouth
Phatnitic Mouth (Damietta Mouth)

(Rosetta)•

Damietta •

(Abukir) •
•Buto

Mendesic Mou
Tanitic M

Lake
Menzaleh

(Alexandria) •

Thmuis •
• Mendes

Heracleopo
Parva

Sin.
Pelus

31°

Lake
Mareotis

Damanhur•

(Naucratis) •

Sebennytos •
Busiris •

Raamses?, Zoan,
Tanis, (San)

Tahpanhes, Daphnae•
Baal-zephon?

Sile
Eth

E G Y P T

Raamses ?
(Faqus)
GOSHEN

Lake
Balah

Zagazig
Bubastis •

Pithom, Heroonpolis
OF (Tell Ertabeh)

Isma

B

(Bilbeis)

LAND

Theku, Succoth?
(Tell el Mashkhuta)

La
Tin

Great
Bitter
Lake

•Heliopolis, On

30°

• (Cairo)

Gizeh •
Abusir △

JEBEL ATAQA
(S

Kh

Saqqara △
Dahshur △
(PYRAMIDS)

• Memphis, Noph

Lisht △

C

Lake
Moeris

(EL FAIYUM)

Crocodilopolis •

Heracleopolis Magna
• (Hanesh?)

**EGYPT AND LANDS
OF THE EXODUS**
(13th Century B.C.)

———— Traditional Route to Sinai

•-•-•-•- Possible first legs of the Traditional Route

- - - - Continuations of the Traditional Route
from Sinai to Kadesh-barnea

-○-○-○- Theory of a journey to an Arabian Sinai

———— Northern Route

•-•-•-• Alternate possibilities of the Northern Route

-○-○-○- Possible route of a delegation from
Kadesh-barnea to Sinai

- - - - Probable route of wanderings from
Kadesh-barnea to Canaan

———— Possible alternate route of wanderings
from Kadesh-barnea to Canaan

▨ Fertile land

⊔⊔ Indefinite
Boundaries

Gizeh Modern names
underlined

Scale: 0   25   50   75 miles

Copyright by Rand McNally & Company

D

• (Oxyrhynchus)

• (Beni Hasan)

28°

• Hermopolis

E

• Ekhet-Aton
(Tell el Amarna)

Thebes
↓

16

MAP V

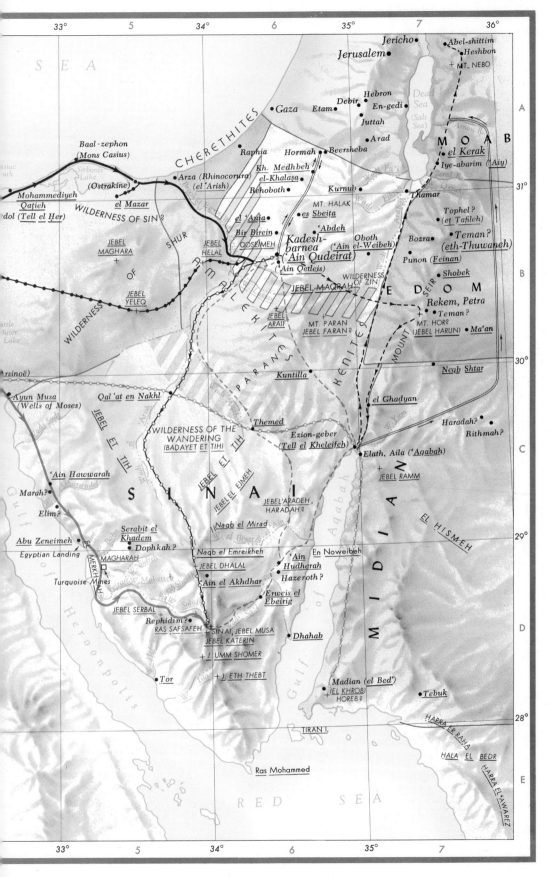

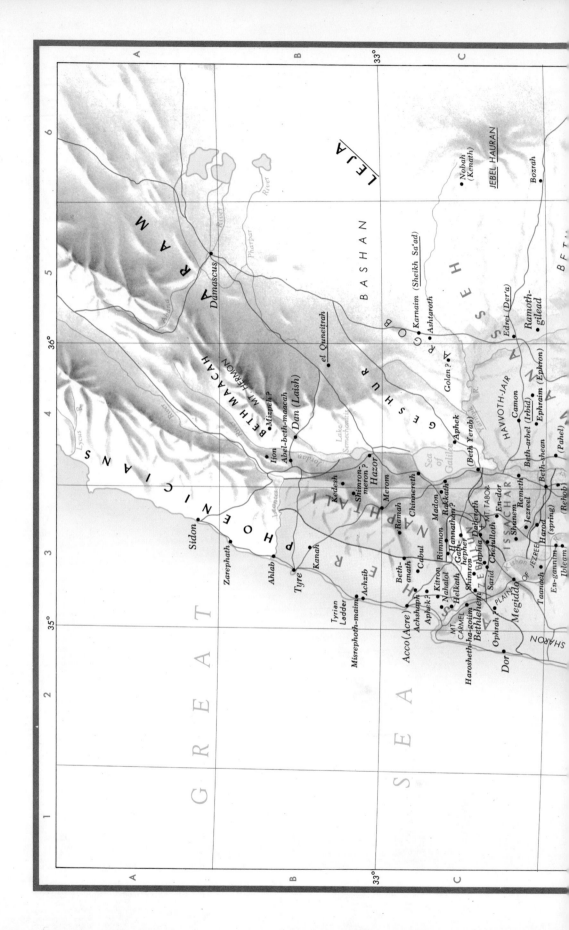

MAP VI

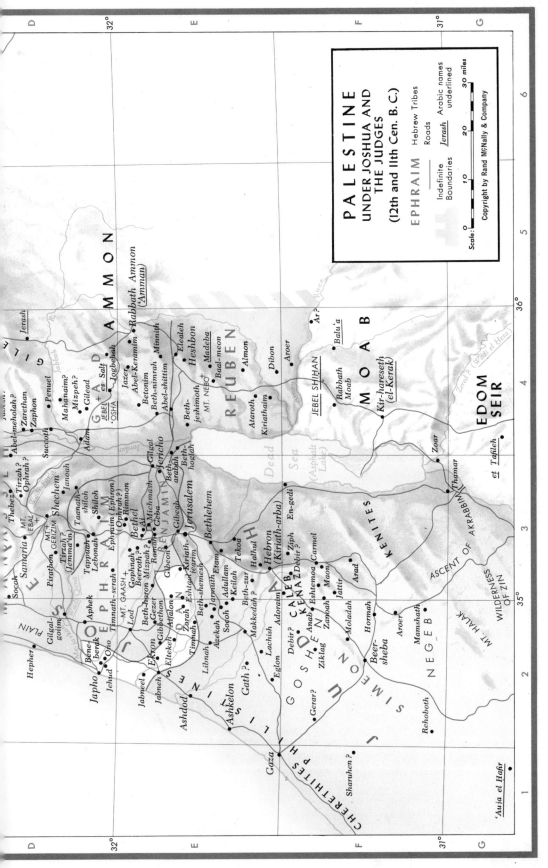

PALESTINE
UNDER JOSHUA AND
THE JUDGES
(12th and 11th Cen. B. C.)

EPHRAIM Hebrew Tribes
            Roads
Jerash Arabic names
            underlined

Indefinite
Boundaries

Scale: 0   10   20   30 miles

Copyright by Rand McNally & Company

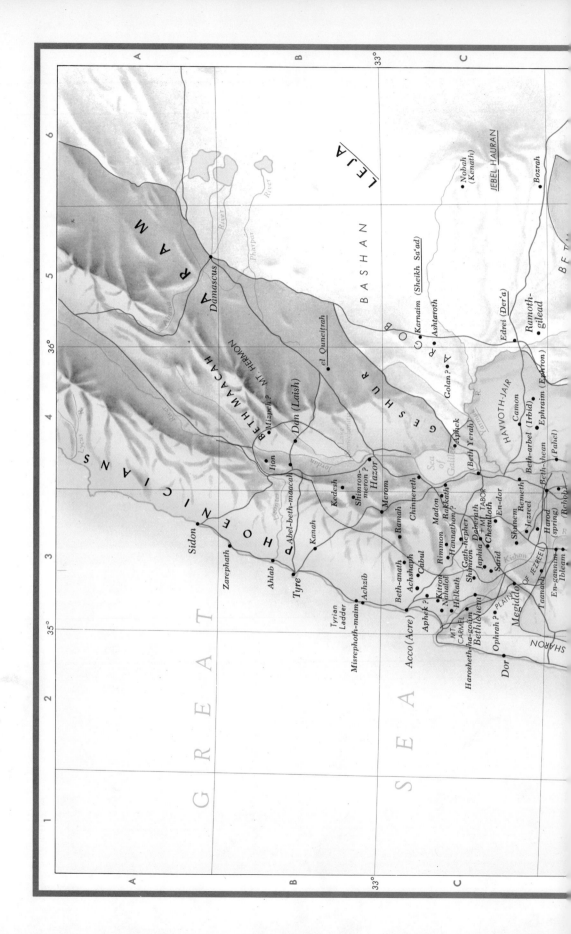

20

MAP VII

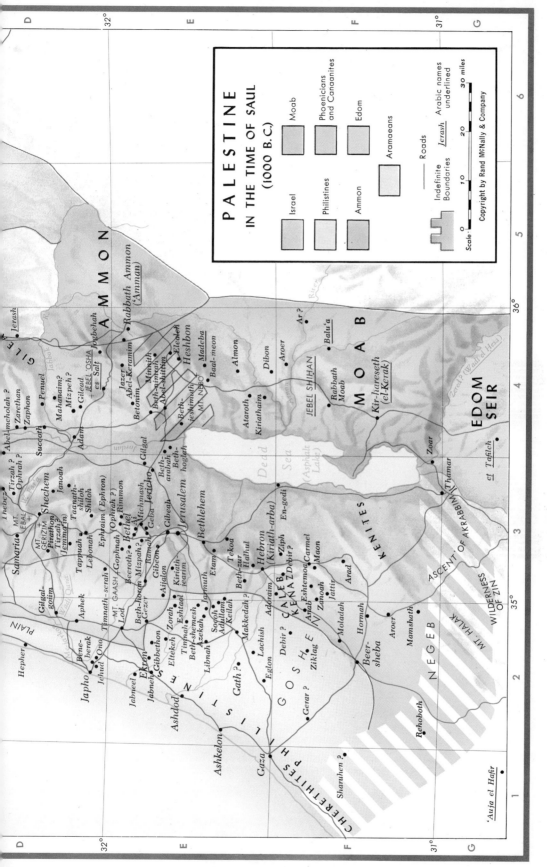

PALESTINE
IN THE TIME OF SAUL
(1000 B.C.)

Israel
Moab

Philistines
Phoenicians
and Canaanites

Ammon
Edom

Aramaeans

Indefinite
Boundaries
Roads
Jerash   Arabic names
underlined

Scale
0   10   20   30 miles
Copyright by Rand McNally & Company

Jerash

GILEAD

AMMON

Rabbath Ammon
(Amman)

Jogbehah
JEBEL OSHA
es-Salt
Gilead
Mizpeh?
Mahanaim?

Penuel
Zaphon
Zarethan
Abel-meholah?
Tirzah? Ophrah?
Thebez

Samaria?
MT. EBAL
MT. GERIZIM
Shechem
Pirathon
Tirzah?
(Temma'in)
Taanath-
shiloh
Janoah
Lebonah
Tappuah
Beeroth?
Gophnah (Ophrah?)
Ephraim (Ephron?)
Bethel
Ramah

Jazer
Abel-keramim
Betonim
Mimrath
Abel-shittim
Beth-
jeshimoth
MT. NEBO

Eleaeh
Heshbon
Madeba
Baal-meon
Almon
Dibon
Aroer

Ar?
Batu'a

JEBEL SHIHAN

Rabbath
Moab
Kir-hareseth
(el-Karak)

M O A B

Ataroth
Kiriathaim

Gilgal

Beth-
arabah
Beth-
hoglah

Michmash?
Geba Jericho
Gibeah
Jerusalem

Rimmon

Bethlehem

Tekoa
Beth-zur
Halhul
Hebron
(Kiriath-arba)
Debir?
Carmel
Maon
Ziph

En-gedi

Dead
Sea
(Asphalt
Lake)

Zoar

et-Tafileh
Thamar

EDOM
SEIR

Zered R. (Wadi'el Hesa)
Arnon River

Hepher

PLAIN

Gilgal-
goiim
Aphek
Bene-
berak
Jehud Ono?
Japho
Jabneel
Jabneh
Ekron
Gibbethon
Ashdod
Ashkelon
Gaza

MT. GAASH?
Beth-horon Mizpah?
Gibeon
Aijalon
Gezer
Kiriath-
jearim
Zorah
Eltekeh
Timnah
Beth-shemesh
Azekah
Libnah
Lachish
Eglon
Gath?
Timnath-serah
Lod

Jarmuth
Socoh
Adullam
Keilah
Makkedah?
Adoraim

G O S H E N
Gerar?
Ziklag

Etam

Beth-zur

Debir?
Eshtemoa
Anab
Zanoah
Jattir

Arad

Moladah
Hormah

Beer-
sheba

Aroer

Mamshath

Rehoboth

Sharuhen?

'Auja el Hafr

NEGEB

WILDERNESS
OF ZIN
MT. HALAK
ASCENT OF AKRABBIM

KENITES

CALEB
KENAZ

C H E R E T H I T E S
P H I L I S T I N E S

21

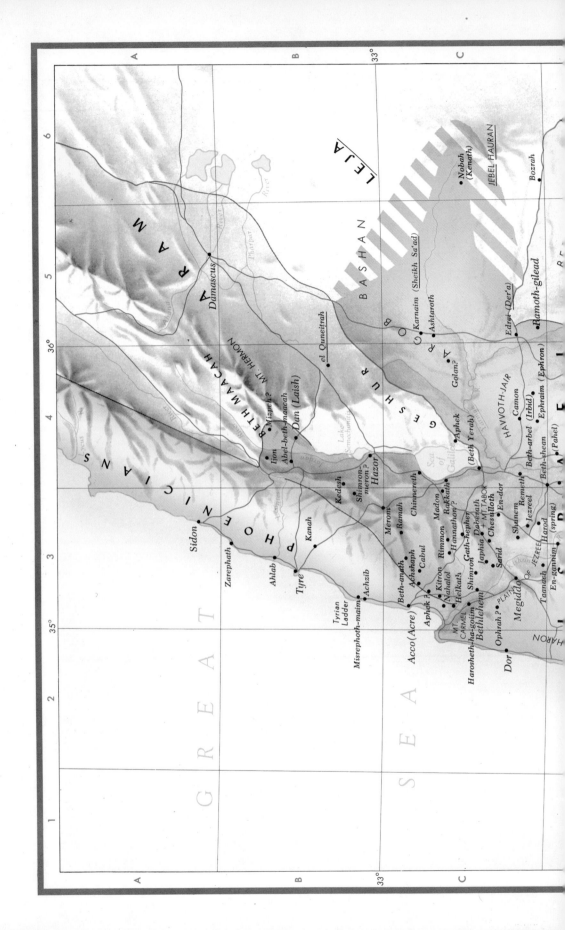

A B 33° C

6

LEJA

BASHAN

• Nobah
(Kenath)

JEBEL HAURAN

• Bozrah

5

A
R
A
M

Damascus

Pharpar River

el Quneitrah

• Karnaim (Sheikh Sa'ad)
• Ashtaroth
Golan?

• Edrei (Der'a)

Ramoth-gilead

B
A
S
H
A
N

36°

MT. HERMON

Ijon
Abel-beth-maacah
Dan (Laish)
Mizpeh?

BETH MAACAH

G
E
S
H
U
R

Aphek

(Beth Yerah)

HAVVOTH-JAIR

• Camon

Beth-arbel (Irbid)
• Ephraim (Ephron)

• Beth-shean

4

P
H
O
E
N
I
C
I
A
N
S

Kedesh

Shimron?
meron?
Hazor

Merom
Chinnereth
Madon
Rakkath
Hannathon?
Ramah

Lake
Semachonitis

Sea
of
Galilee

Beth-arbel (Irbid)
Ephraim (Ephron)
• Pahel

GILEAD

3

Sidon

Zarephath

Ahlab

Kanah

Tyre

Beth-anath
Achshaph
Cabul
Kitron
Nahalal
Helkath
Shimron
Rimmon
Dabenath
MT. TABOR
Chesulloth
Iaphia
Shunem
En-dor
Remeth
Jezreel
Guth-hepher
Sarid

PLAIN

2

G R E A T

Achzib

Tyrian
Ladder

Misrephoth-maim

Acco (Acre)
Aphek?

Haroseth-ha-goiim

Bethlehem
Ophrah?
MT.
CARMEL
Megiddo
Taanach
En-gannim
Harod
OF
JEZREEL
(spring)

Dor

SHARON

1

S E A

A

B

33°

C

MAP VIII

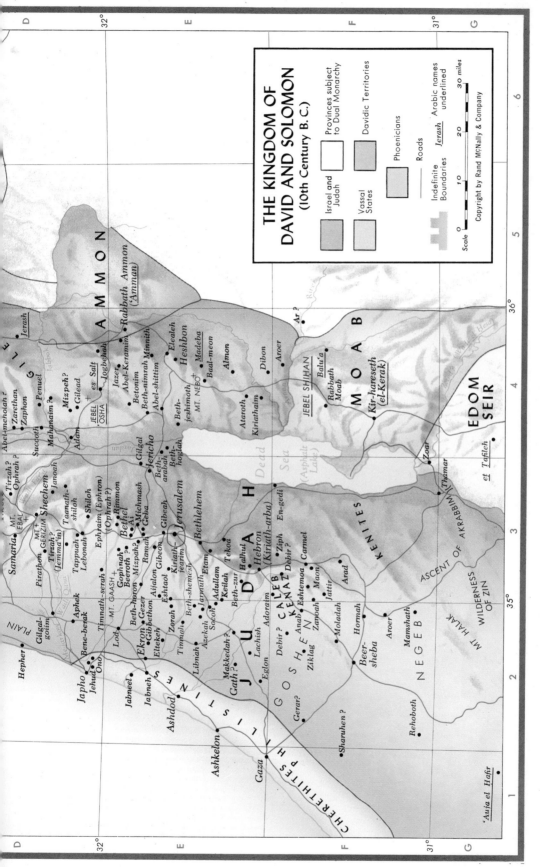

THE KINGDOM OF
DAVID AND SOLOMON
(10th Century B.C.)

Provinces subject
to Dual Monarchy

Davidic Territories

Phoenicians

Roads

Israel and
Judah

Vassal
States

Indefinite
Boundaries

Jerash Arabic names
underlined

Scale

0   10   20   30 miles

Copyright by Rand McNally & Company

GILEAD

AMMON

Jerash

Rabbath Ammon
('Ammon)

es Salt

Jogbehah

Penuel

Mizpeh?

Gilead

Jazer

Abel-Keramim

Minnith

Elealeh

Heshbon

Madeba

Baal-meon

Almon

JEBEL
'OSHA

Mahanaim?

Zaphon

Zarethan

Abel-meholah?

Succoth

Adam

Betonim

Beth-nimrah

Abel-shittim

Beth-
jeshimoth

MT. NEBO

Kiriathaim

Ataroth

Dibon

Aroer

Ar?

JEBEL SHIHAN

Balu'a

Rabbath
Moab

MOAB

Kir-hareseth
(el-Kerak)

EDOM
SEIR

et Tafileh

Zoar

Thamar

ASCENT OF AKRABBIM

KENITES

Dead

Sea

(Asphalt
Lake)

En-gedi

Tirzah?

Ophrah?

Samaria

MT.
EBAL

MT.
GERIZIM

Shechem

Pirathon

Tirzah?
(Jemma'in)

Janoah

Tappuah

Ephraim (Ophrah?)

Shiloh

Lebonah

Taanath-
shiloh

Gilgal

Jericho

Beth-
arabah

Beth-
hoglah

Bethel

Ai

Rimmon

Michmash

Ramah

Beeroth?

Gibeon

Gibeah

Geba

Mizpah?

Gophnah?

MT. GAASH

Beth-horon

Gezer

Aijalon

Kiriath-
jearim

Jerusalem

Bethlehem

Tekoa

Etam

Beth-zur

Adullam

Keilah

Jarmuth

Beth-shemesh

Sochoh

Azekah

Adoraim

Hebron (Kiriath-arba)

Halhul

Ziph

Maon

Carmel

Debir?

Debir?

Anab

Eshtemoa

Jattir

Arad

CALEB
KENAZ

JUDAH

GOSHEN

Zanoah

Moladah

Hormah

Aroer

Mamshath

Beer-
sheba

NEGEB

MT HALAK

WILDERNESS
OF ZIN

Rehoboth

Sharuhen?

Gaza

Gerar?

Eglon

Lachish

Libnah

Makkedah?

Gath?

Timnah

Zorah

Eltekeh

Ekron

Eshtaol

Ashkelon

Ashdod

Jabneh

Jabneel

Loth

Ono

Jehud

Japho

Aphek

Bene-berak

Gibbethon

Timnath-serah

Hepher

Gilgal-
goiim

PLAIN

CHERETHITES
PHILISTINES

'Auja el Hafir

23

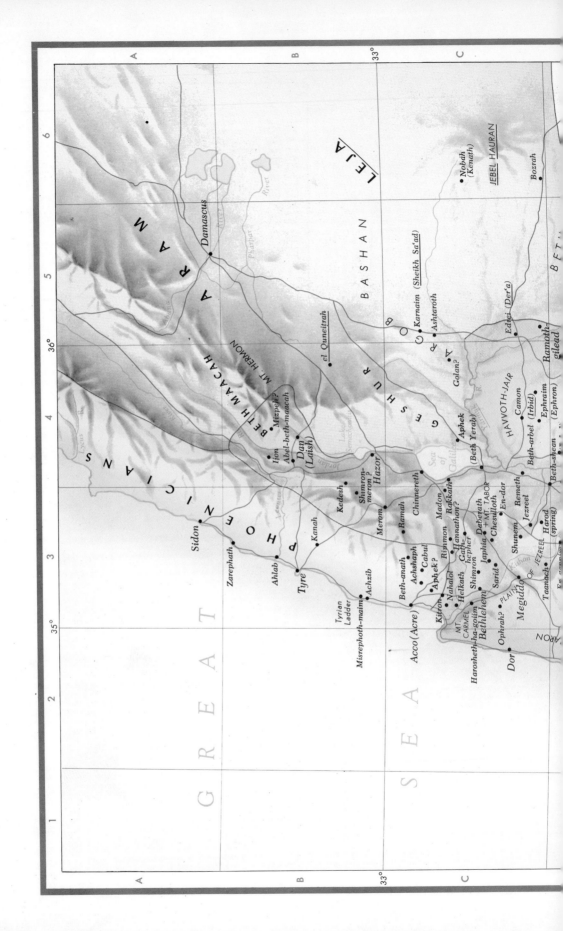

24

A   B   33°   C

6   5   36°   4   35°   3   2   1

A R A M

Damascus

Pharpar River

Abana River

LEJA

JEBEL HAURAN

Nobah (Kenath)

Bozrah

BASHAN

el Quneitrah

Karnaim (Sheikh Sa'ad)

Ashtaroth

G E S H U R

Golan?

Edrei (Dera)

Ramoth-gilead

MT. HERMON

BETH-MAACAH

Ijon   Mizpeh?
Abel-beth-maacah
Dan (Laish)

Aphek (Beth Yerah)

HAVVOTH-JAIR

Camon

Beth-arbel (Irbid)

Ephron (Ephron)

BET

PHOENICIANS

Sidon

Zarephath

Ahlab

Tyre

Kanah

Kedesh

Shimron-meron

Hazor

Chinnereth

Sea of Galilee

Lake Semechonitis

Jordan River

Leontes River

Lycus River

Madon

Rakkath

Hannathon?

Remeth

Beth-shean

Merom

Ramah

Rimmon

Gath-hepher

Daberath
MT. TABOR
Chesulloth

En-dor

Jezreel

Shunem

Harod (spring)

Tyrian Ladder

Misrephoth-maim

Achzib

Beth-anath

Achshaph

Cabul

Aphek?

Nahalol
Helkath?

Shimron

Iphtah

Sarid

Kishon River

PLAIN OF JEZREEL

Acco (Acre)

Kitron

Bethlehem

Ophrah?

Megiddo

Taanach

En-gannim

Dor

MT. CARMEL

Harosheth-ha-goiim

SHARON

G R E A T   S E A

A   B   33°   C

MAP IX

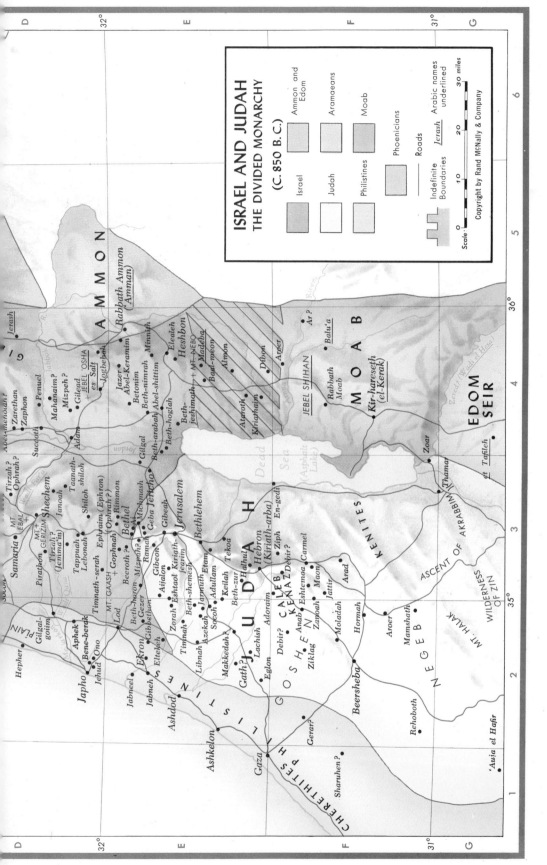

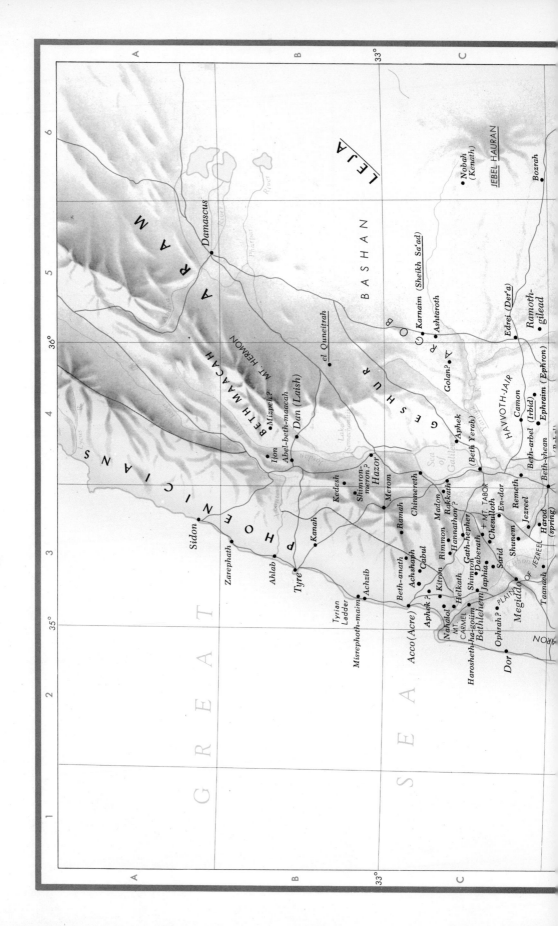

26

MAP X

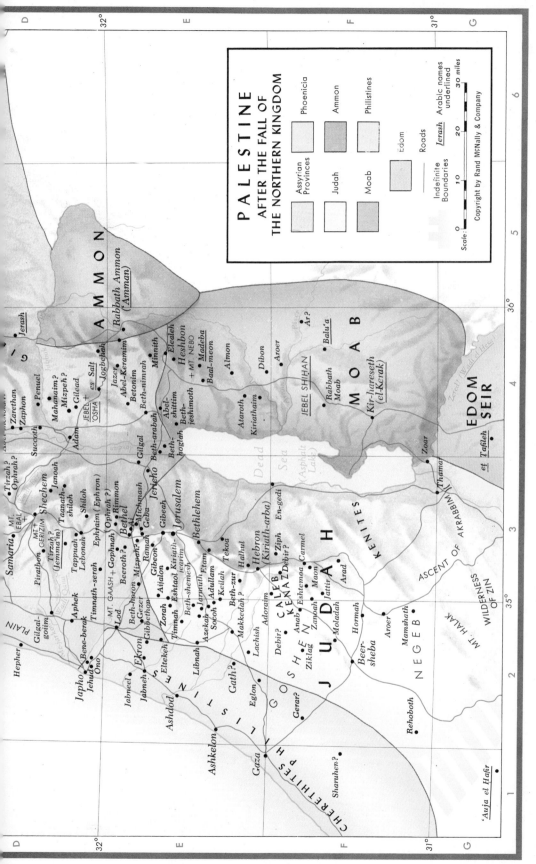

PALESTINE
AFTER THE FALL OF
THE NORTHERN KINGDOM

Assyrian Provinces | Phoenicia
Judah | Ammon
Moab | Philistines
Edom
Indefinite Boundaries | Roads
Jerash Arabic names underlined

Scale: 0 10 20 30 miles

Copyright by Rand McNally & Company

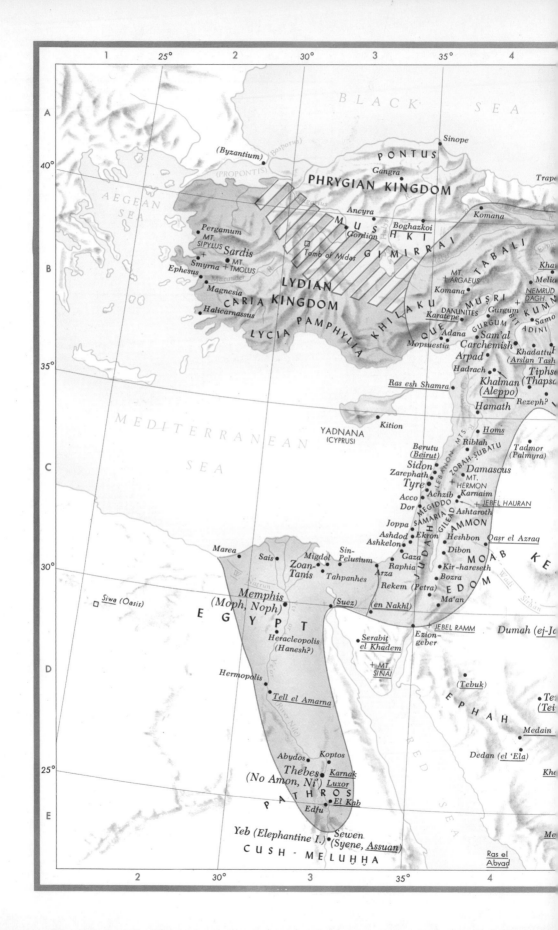

28

Top coordinates: 1 25° 2 30° 3 35° 4

BLACK SEA

Sinope

PONTUS

(Byzantium)
(PROPONTIS)
Boshorus

Gangra

PHRYGIAN KINGDOM

Trape

AEGEAN SEA

Ancyra

Komana

M U S H K I

Boghazkoi

Pergamum
MT. SIPYLUS
Sardis

Gordion
Tomb of Midas

G I M I R R A I

MT. ARGAEUS

Kha

Smyrna MT. TMOLUS

T A B A L I

Melia

Ephesus

Komana

NEMRUD DAGH.

Magnesia

LYDIAN KINGDOM

MUŞRI

KUMM

Halicarnassus

CARIA

K H I L A K U

DANUNITES

Karatepe

Gurgum

Samo

ADINI

LYCIA PAMPHYLIA

QUE

Adana

GURGUM

Sam'al

Mopsuestia

Carchemish

Khadattu

Arpad

(Arslan Tash

Ras esh Shamra

Hadrach

Tiphse

Khalman

(Thapsa

(Aleppo)

Kition

Hamath

Rezeph?

YADNANA
(CYPRUS)

Homs

Tadmor
(Palmyra)

M E D I T E R R A N E A N

Berutu
(Beirut)

Riblah

ZOBAH-SUBATU

S E A

Sidon

Zarephath

Damascus

MT. HERMON

Tyre

Karnaim

Acco

Achzib

+ JEBEL HAURAN

Dor

Megiddo

Ashtaroth

Joppa

SAMARIA GILEAD

AMMON

Marea

Sais

Migdol

Sin-
Pelusium

Ashdod Ekron

Heshbon

Qaşr el Azraq

Zoan-
Tanis

Gaza

Ashkelon

Dibon

MOAB

KE

Tahpanhes

Raphia

Kir-hareseth

Siwa (Oasis)

Arza

Bozra

Memphis
(Moph, Noph)

(Suez)

Rekem (Petra)

EDOM

E G Y P T

(en Nakhl)

Ma'an

Dumah (ej-Jo

Heracleopolis
(Hanesh?)

Serabit
el Khadem

Ezion-
geber

+ JEBEL RAMM

Hermopolis

+ MT. SINAI

E P H A H

(Tebuk)

Te
(Tei

Tell el Amarna

Medain

Dedan (el 'Ela)

Abydos

Koptos

Thebes
(No Amon, Ni')

Karnak

Luxor

Kh

P A T H R O S

El Kab

Edfu

Yeb (Elephantine I.)

Sewen
(Syene, Assuan)

Me

C U S H - M E L U H H A

Ras el
Abyad

Bottom coordinates: 2 30° 3 35° 4

MAP XI

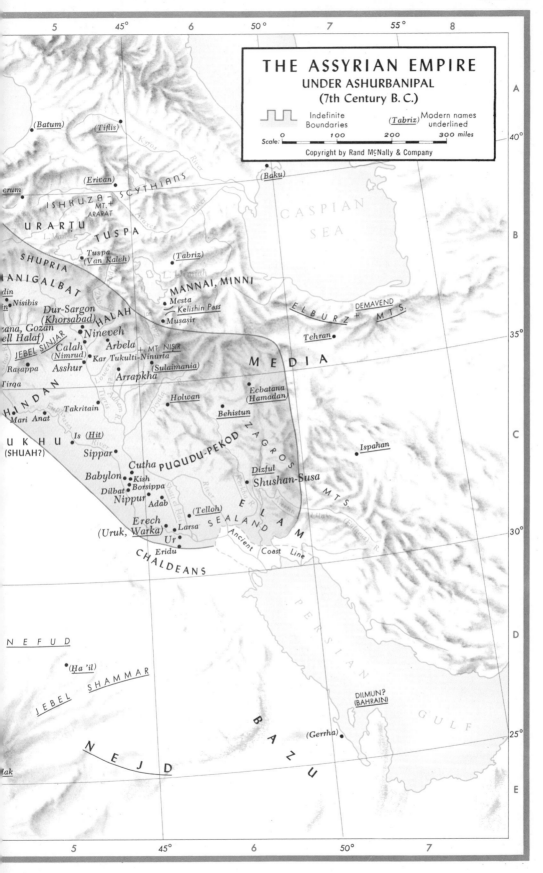

THE ASSYRIAN EMPIRE
UNDER ASHURBANIPAL
(7th Century B.C.)

Indefinite Boundaries

Tabriz Modern names underlined

Scale: 0   100   200   300 miles

Copyright by Rand McNally & Company

(Batum)

(Tiflis)

(Erivan)

erum

ISHKUZA SCYTHIANS

MT. ARARAT

URARTU

TUSPA

SHUPRIA

din

Nisibis

HANIGALBAT

Tuspa (Van Kaleh)

(Tabriz)

(Baku)

CASPIAN SEA

MANNAI, MINNI

Mesta

Kelishin Pass

Muṣaṣir

Dur-Sargon (Khorsabad)

HALAH

Nineveh

zana, Gozan (ell Halaf)

JEBEL SINJAR

Calah (Nimrud)

Arbela

MT. NIṢIR

Kar Tukulti-Ninurta

Raṣappa

Asshur

(Sulaimania)

Tirqa

Arrapkha

HINDAN

Takritain

Mari Anat

Holwan

Behistun

Ecbatana (Hamadan)

Tehran

ELBURZ MTS.

DEMAVEND

MEDIA

Ispahan

UKHU (SHUAH?)

Is (Hit)

Sippar

Cutha

PUQUDU-PEKOD

Babylon

Kish

Dilbat

Borsippa

Nippur

Adab

Erech (Uruk, Warka)

Larsa

(Telloh)

Ur

Eridu

Dizful

Shushan-Susa

ELAM

ZAGROS MTS.

SEALAND

Ancient Coast Line

CHALDEANS

NEFUD

(Ḥa'il)

JEBEL SHAMMAR

DILMUN? (BAHRAIN)

BAZU

(Gerrha)

PERSIAN GULF

NEJD

lak

29

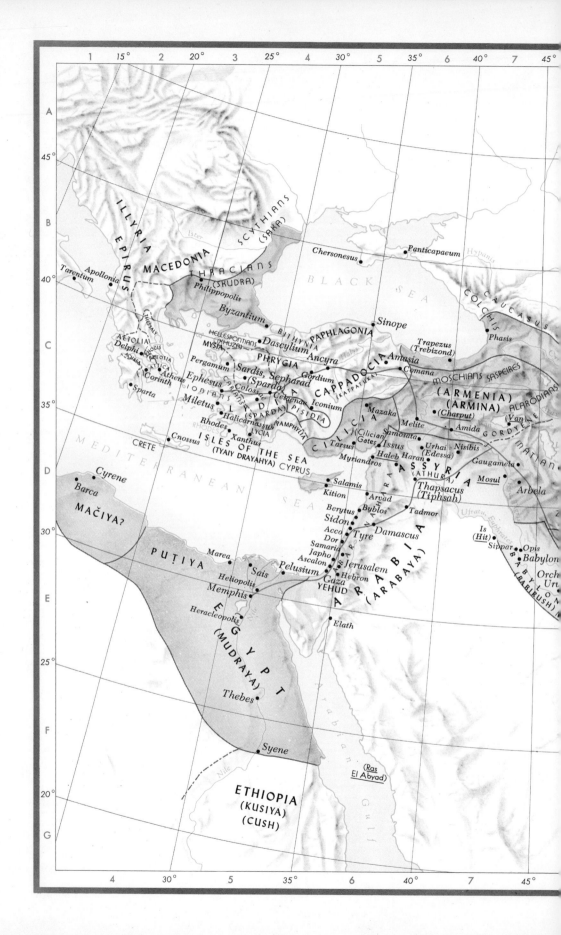

Map labels (grid coordinates top): 1 15° 2 20° 3 25° 4 30° 5 35° 6 40° 7 45°

Row labels: A 45° B 40° C 35° D 30° E 25° F 20° G

Bottom labels: 4 30° 5 35° 6 40° 7 45°

ILLYRIA
EPIRUS
MACEDONIA
SCYTHIANS
(SAKA)
THRACIANS
(SKUDRA)
Ister
Tarentum
Apollonia
Philippopolis
Byzantium
Chersonesus
Panticapaeum
Hypanis
BLACK SEA
CAUCASUS
COLCHIS
Sinope
Phasis
Trapezus
(Trebizond)
BITHYNIA
PAPHLAGONIA
Daseylium
Ancyra
Amasia
Comana
HELLESPONTIANS
(TUHUZA)
PHRYGIA
MOSCHIANS SASPEIRES
MYSIA
AETOLIAI
Delphi
PHOCIS
BOEOTIA
ATTICA
Athens
Corinth
Pergamum
Sardis, Sepharad
(Sparda)
Gordium
CAPPADOCIA
(KATPATUKA)
(ARMENIA)
(ARMINA)
ALARODIANS
Mazaka
(Charput)
Ephesus
Colosse
Iconium
Melite
(Van)
GORDYENE
CARIA
LYDIA
(SPARDA)
Samosata
Amida
MATIAN
Miletus
PISIDIA
CILICIA
Cilician
Gates
Issus
Urhai
(Edessa)
Nisibis
Sparta
Halicarnassus
Cnossus
Xanthus
LYCIA
PAMPHYLIA
Tarsus
Haleb
Haran
Gaugamela
Mosul
Rhodes
RHODES
ISLES OF THE SEA
(TYAIY DRAYAHYA) CYPRUS
Myriandros
ASSYRIA
(ATHURA)
Arbela
CRETE
MEDITERRANEAN SEA
Salamis
Kition
Arvad
Thapsacus
(Tiphsah)
Ufratu
Euphrates
Cyrene
Barca
Berytus
Byblos
Tadmor
Is
(Hit)
Opis
Sippar
Babylon
MAČIYA?
Sidon
Acco
Dor
Tyre
Damascus
ARABIA
(ARABAYA)
BABYLON
(BABIRUSH)
Orch
Uru
Marea
Samaria
Japho
Ascalon
Jerusalem
Hebron
PUTIYA
Sais
Pelusium
Gaza
YEHUD
Heliopolis
Memphis
EGYPT
(MUDRAYA)
Elath
Heracleopolis
Nile
Thebes
Arabian Gulf
Syene
(Ras
El Abyad)
Nile
ETHIOPIA
(KUSIYA)
(CUSH)

MAP XII

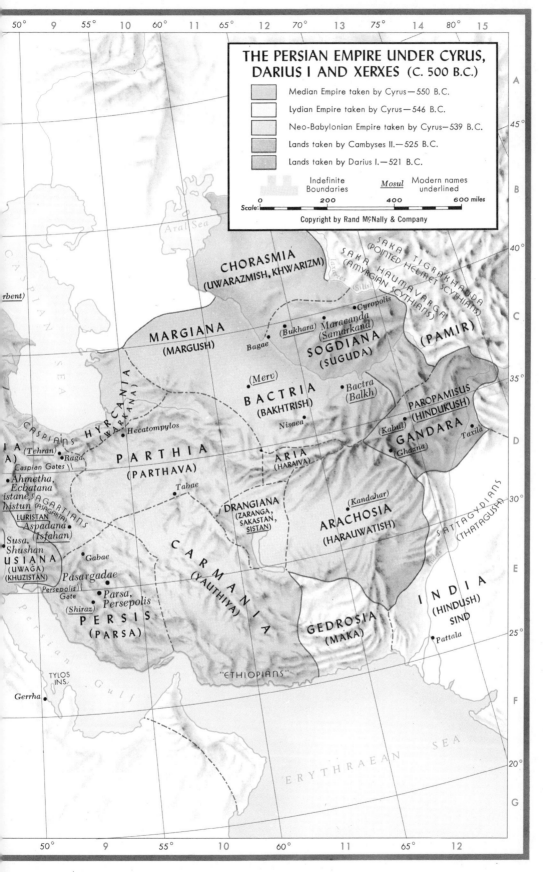

Median Empire taken by Cyrus—550 B.C.

Lydian Empire taken by Cyrus—546 B.C.

Neo-Babylonian Empire taken by Cyrus—539 B.C.

Lands taken by Cambyses II.—525 B.C.

Lands taken by Darius I.—521 B.C.

Indefinite Boundaries   *Mosul*   Modern names underlined

Scale: 0   200   400   600 miles

Copyright by Rand McNally & Company

Aral Sea

rbent)

CHORASMIA
(UWARAZMISH, KHWARIZM)

SAKA TIGRAKHAUDA
(POINTED HELMET SCYTHIANS)

SAKA HAUMAVARGA
(AMYRGIAN SCYTHIANS)

Iaxartes

(Silis)

•Cyropolis

MARGIANA
(MARGUSH)

•(Bukhara)   •Maracanda
(Samarkand)

Bagae

SOGDIANA
(SUGUDA)

(PAMIR)

CASPIAN   SEA

•(Merv)

BACTRIA
(BAKHTRISH)

•Bactra
(Balkh)

PAROPAMISUS
(HINDUKUSH)

HYRCANIA
(WARKANA)

•Hecatompylos

Nisaea

•(Kabul)   GANDARA

•Taxila

A)   •(Tehran)

•(Raga)

PARTHIA
(PARTHAVA)

ARIA
(HARAIVA)

•(Ghazna)

Caspian Gates

•Ahmetha,
Echatana
istane
histun

SAGARTIANS
(ASAGARTA)

Tabae

DRANGIANA
(ZARANGA,
SAKASTAN,
SISTAN)

•(Kandahar)

ARACHOSIA
(HARAUWATISH)

SATTAGYDIANS
(THATAGUSH)

LURISTAN

Aspadana
•(Isfahan)

•Susa,
Shushan

USIANA
(UWAĞA)
(KHUZISTAN)

•Gabae

CARMANIA
(YAUTHIYA)

Pasargadae

•Persepolis
Gate

•Parsa,
Persepolis

INDIA
(HINDUSH)
SIND

(Shiraz)

PERSIS
(PARSA)

GEDROSIA
(MAKA)

•Pattala

Persian Gulf

TYLOS
INS.

"ETHIOPIANS"

Gerrha•

ERYTHRAEAN   SEA

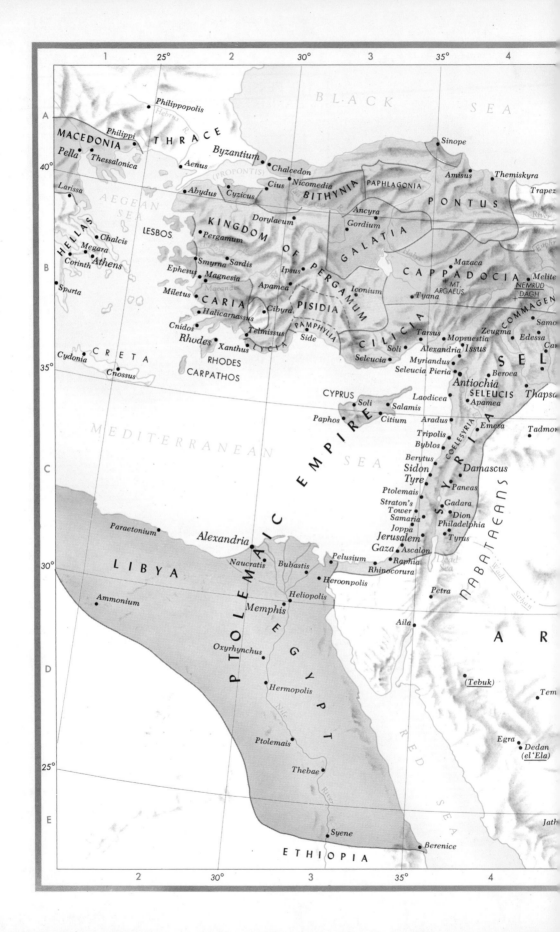

32

MAP XIII

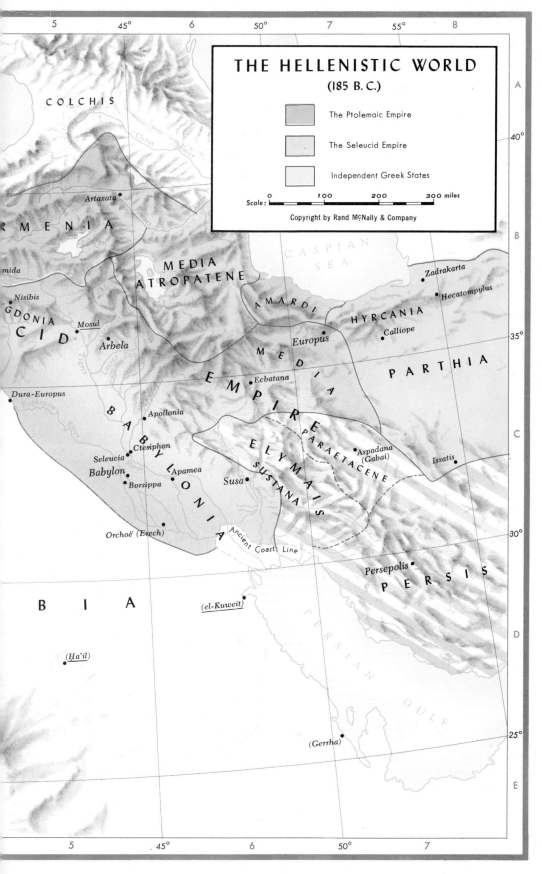

THE HELLENISTIC WORLD
(185 B. C.)

The Ptolemaic Empire

The Seleucid Empire

Independent Greek States

Scale: 0   100   200   300 miles

Copyright by Rand McNally & Company

COLCHIS

Artaxata

RMENIA

mida

Nisibis

GDONIA

CID

Mosul

Arbela

MEDIA
ATROPATENE

AMARDI

CASPIAN
SEA

Zadrakarta

Hecatompylus

HYRCANIA

Calliope

Europus

M
E
D
I
A

PARTHIA

Dura-Europus

Ecbatana

EMPIRE

Apollonia

B
A
B
Y
L
O
N
I
A

Ctesiphon

Seleucia

Babylon

Apamea

Borsippa

Susa

ELYMAIS

SUSIANA

PARAETACENE

Aspadana
(Gabai)

Issatis

Orchoë (Erech)

Ancient Coast Line

Persepolis

P E R S I S

B I A

(el-Kuweit)

(Ha'il)

P
E
R
S
I
A
N

G
U
L
F

(Gerrha)

33

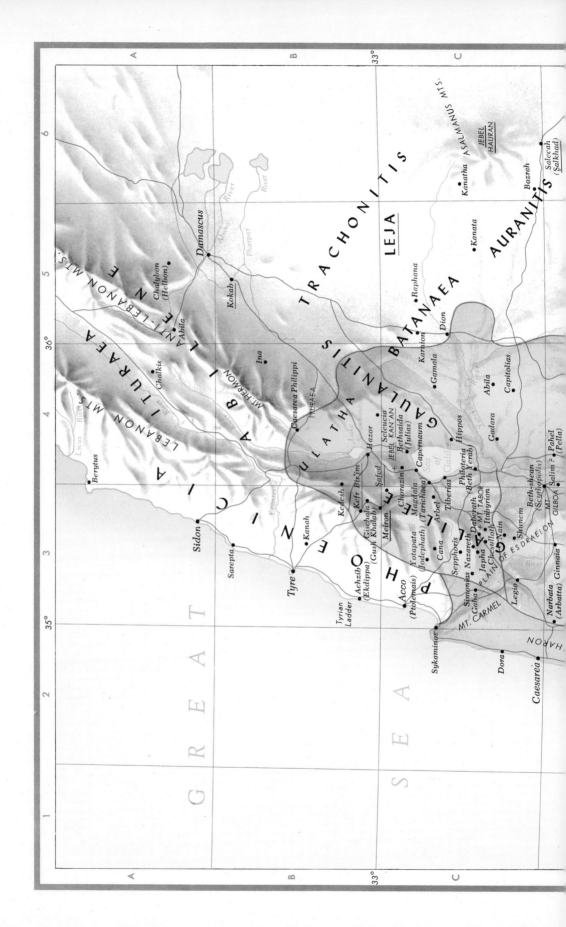

MAP XIV

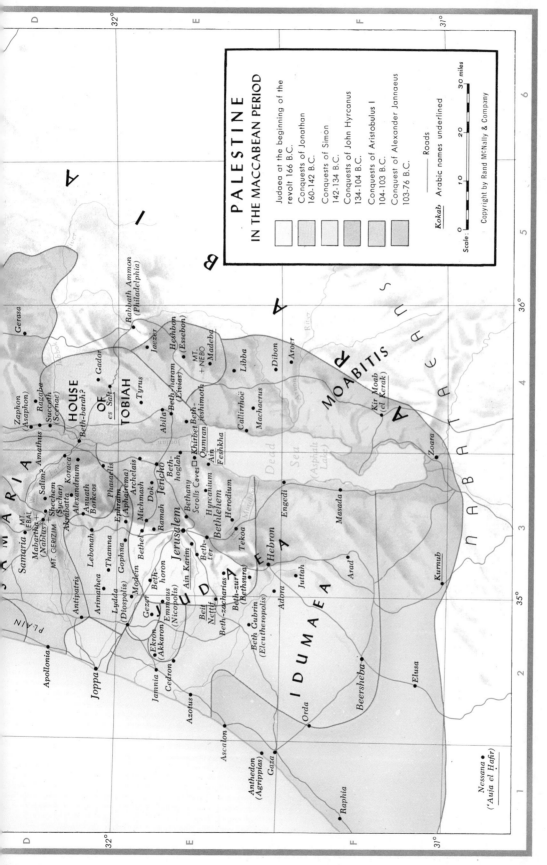

PALESTINE
IN THE MACCABEAN PERIOD

Judaea at the beginning of the
revolt 166 B.C.

Conquests of Jonathan
160-142 B.C.

Conquests of Simon
142-134 B.C.

Conquests of John Hyrcanus
134-104 B.C.

Conquests of Aristobulus I
104-103 B.C.

Conquest of Alexander Jannaeus
103-76 B.C.

— Roads

Kokab   Arabic names underlined

Scale: 0   10   20   30 miles

Copyright by Rand McNally & Company

35

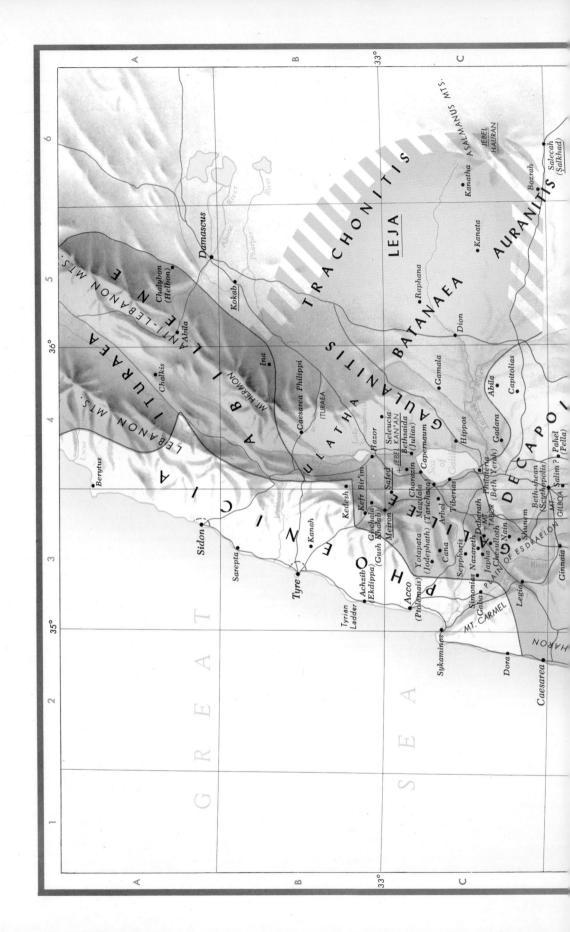

36

A   B   33°   C

6

5

4

36°

3

35°

2

1

GREAT   SEA

ANTI-LEBANON MTS.

LEBANON MTS.

ITURAEA

ABILENE

Chalybon (Helbon)
Abila
Chalkis
Kokab
Ina
Mt HERMON
Damascus

Abana River
Pharpar River

TRACHONITIS

LEJA

BATANAEA

AURANITIS

Jebel HAURAN

ASALMANUS MTS.

Kanatha
Kanata
Raphana
Dion
Bozrah
Salecah (Salkhad)

Caesarea Philippi

ITURAEA

GAULANITIS

ULATHA

Lake Semechonitis

Seleucia
Bethsaida (Julias)
KAN'AN JEBEL
Capernaum
Hazor
Safed
Chorazin
Magdala (Tarichaea)
Arbel
Tiberias
Sea of Galilee

Gamala

Hippos

Abila

Capitolias

Gadara

Yarmuk

DECAPOLIS

Philoteria (Beth Yerah)

Pahel (Pella)

Salim? Beth-shean Scythopolis

Berytus

Kefr Bir'im
Kedesh
Gischala (Gush Halab)
Meiron
Kanah
Yotapata (Jodephath)
Cana
Sepphoris
Simonias
Nazareth Japha
Dabarath +Mt TABOR
Chesulloth
Nain
Shunem

GALILEE

MT. GILBOA

PHOENICIA

Sidon

Sarepta

Tyre

Tyrian Ladder

Achzib (Ekdippa)
Acco (Ptolemais)

Gaba

Sykaminos

MT. CARMEL

PLAIN OF ESDRAELON

Legio

Ginnaia

Dora

Caesarea

SHARON

River

MAP XV

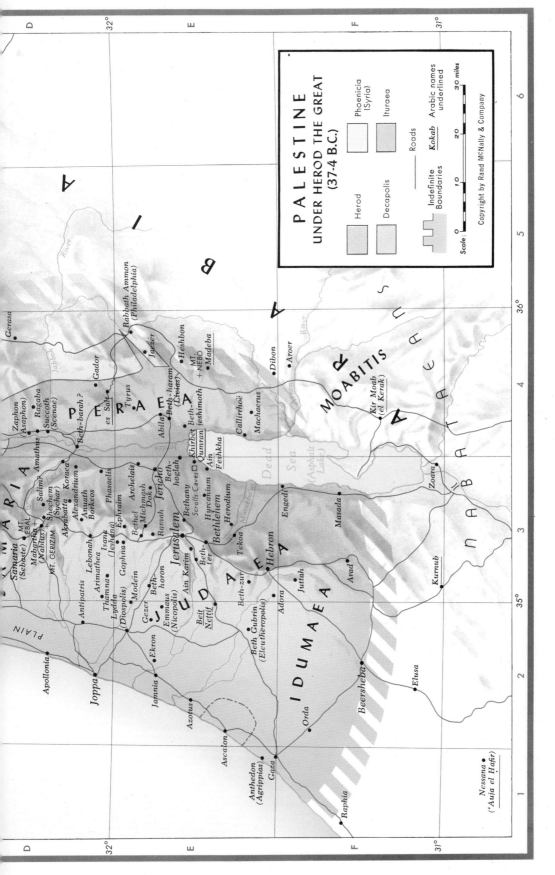

PALESTINE
UNDER HEROD THE GREAT
(37-4 B.C.)

Herod

Decapolis

Phoenicia (Syria)

Ituraea

Roads

Indefinite Boundaries

Kokab Arabic names underlined

Scale: 0   10   20   30 miles

Copyright by Rand McNally & Company

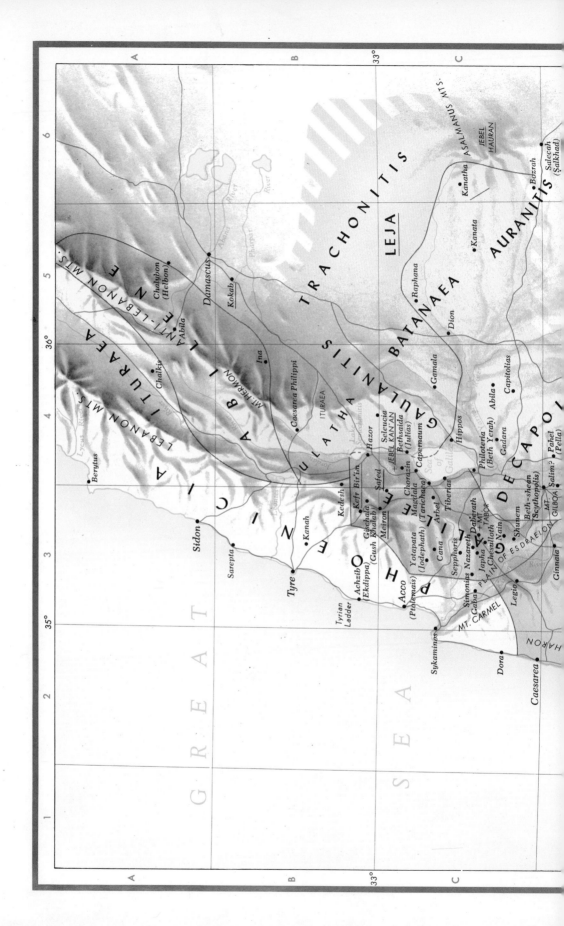

38

MAP XVI

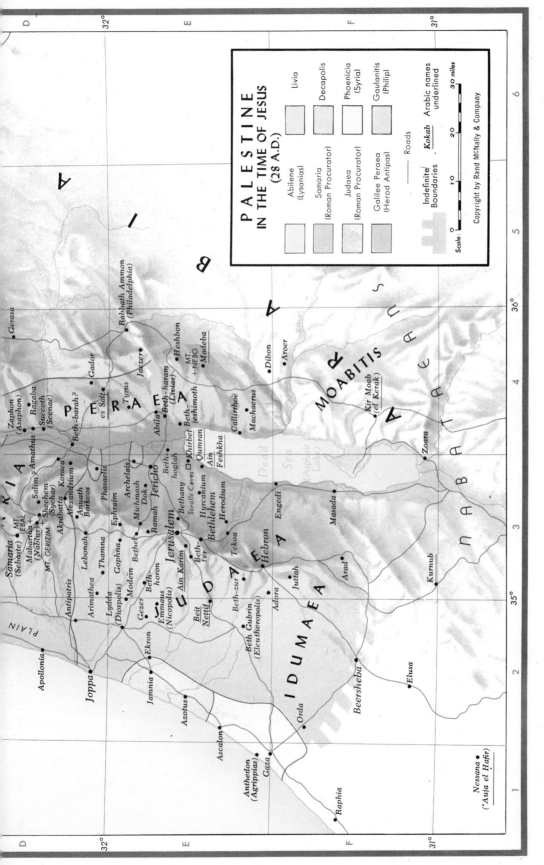

PALESTINE
IN THE TIME OF JESUS
(28 A.D.)

Abilene
(Lysanias)

Samaria
(Roman Procurator)

Judaea
(Roman Procurator)

Galilee Peraea
(Herod Antipas)

Livia

Decapolis

Phoenicia
(Syria)

Gaulanitis
(Philip)

Roads

Indefinite
Boundaries

Kokab Arabic names
underlined

Scale: 0 10 20 30 miles

Copyright by Rand McNally & Company

39

MAP XVII

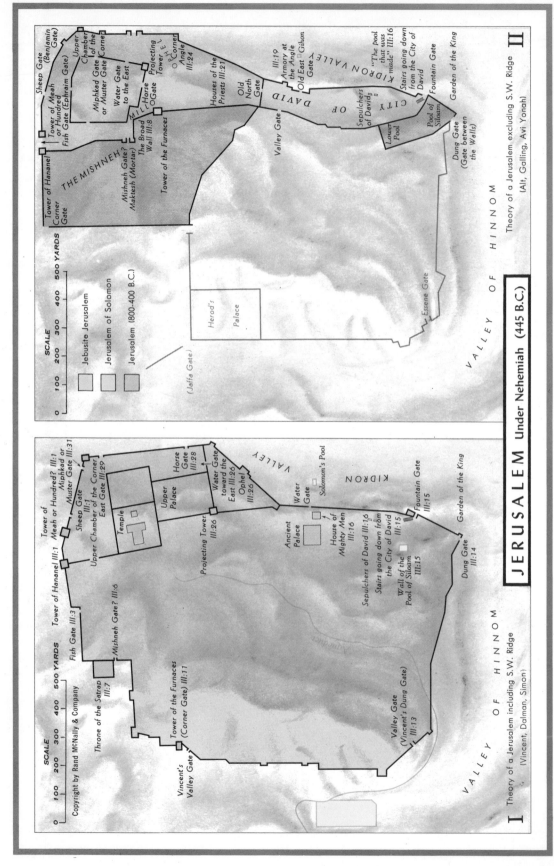

JERUSALEM Under Nehemiah (445 B.C.)

II Theory of a Jerusalem excluding S.W. Ridge
(Alt, Galling, Avi Yonah)

I Theory of a Jerusalem including S.W. Ridge
(Vincent, Dalman, Simon)

Copyright by Rand McNally & Company

40

MAP XVIII

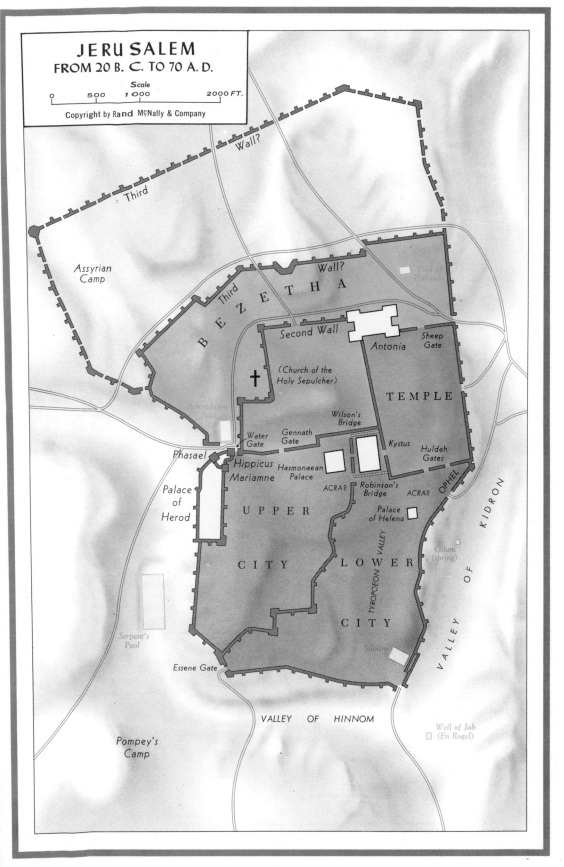

JERUSALEM
FROM 20 B. C. TO 70 A. D.

Scale

0   500   1 000   2000 FT.

Copyright by Rand McNally & Company

Wall?

Third

Assyrian
Camp

B E Z E T H A

Third

Wall?

Pool of
Bethesda

Second Wall

Antonia

Sheep
Gate

✝

(Church of the
Holy Sepulcher)

T E M P L E

Amygdalon
Pool

Wilson's
Bridge

Water
Gate

Gennath
Gate

Kystus

Huldah
Gates

Phasael

Hasmonaean
Palace

Hippicus
Mariamne

ACRA?

Robinson's
Bridge

ACRA?

OPHEL

Palace
of
Herod

U P P E R

Palace
of Helena

C I T Y

L O W E R

Gihon
(spring)

TYROPOEON VALLEY

VALLEY OF KIDRON

C I T Y

Serpent's
Pool

Siloam

Essene Gate

VALLEY OF HINNOM

Well of Job
(En Rogel)

Pompey's
Camp

41

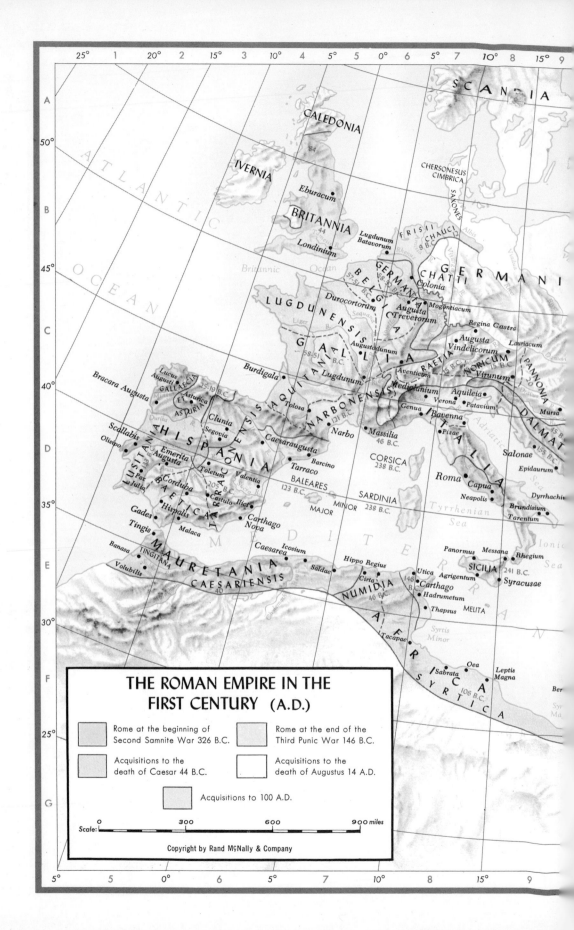

THE ROMAN EMPIRE IN THE FIRST CENTURY (A.D.)

Rome at the beginning of Second Samnite War 326 B.C.

Rome at the end of the Third Punic War 146 B.C.

Acquisitions to the death of Caesar 44 B.C.

Acquisitions to the death of Augustus 14 A.D.

Acquisitions to 100 A.D.

Scale:

0	300	600	900 miles

42

MAP XIX

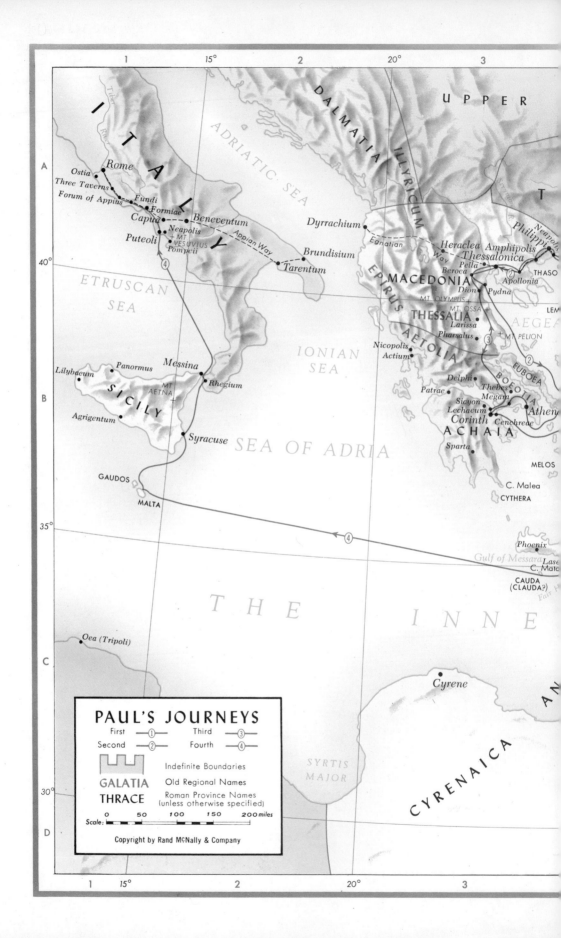

D

15°   2   20°   3

UPPER

ITALY

ADRIATIC SEA

DALMATIA

ILLYRICUM

T

A
Rome
Ostia
Three Taverns
Forum of Appius
Fundi
Formiae
Capua   Beneventum
Neapolis
MT VESUVIUS
Pompeii
Puteoli
Appian Way

Dyrrachium

Egnatian
Way

Neapolis
Philippi
Heraclea Amphipolis
Pella Thessalonica
Beroea   THASO
Apollonia
Pydna

MACEDONIA

Dion

40°

ETRUSCAN

SEA

Brundisium

Tarentum

EPIRUS

MT OLYMPUS
MT OSSA
THESSALIA
Larissa
Pharsalus   MT PELION

AEGEA

LEM

AETOLIA

Nicopolis
Actium

EUBOEA

IONIAN

SEA

Messina

Panormus

MT
AETNA

Rhegium

SICILY

Lilybaeum

Agrigentum

Syracuse

SEA OF ADRIA

Delphi
Patrae
Sicyon
Lechaeum
Corinth Cenchreae
ACHAIA

Thebes
Megara
Athen

BOEOTIA

B

Sparta

MELOS

C. Malea
CYTHERA

GAUDOS

MALTA

Phoenix
Lase
C. Mato

35°

Gulf of Messara

CAUDA
(CLAUDA?)

Fair H

THE

INNE

Oea (Tripoli)

C

Cyrene

PAUL'S JOURNEYS

First —①—   Third —③—
Second —②—   Fourth —④—

Indefinite Boundaries

GALATIA   Old Regional Names

THRACE   Roman Province Names
(unless otherwise specified)

Scale: 0   50   100   150   200 miles

SYRTIS
MAJOR

CYRENAICA

AN

30°

Copyright by Rand McNally & Company

D

15°   2   20°   3

44

MAP XX

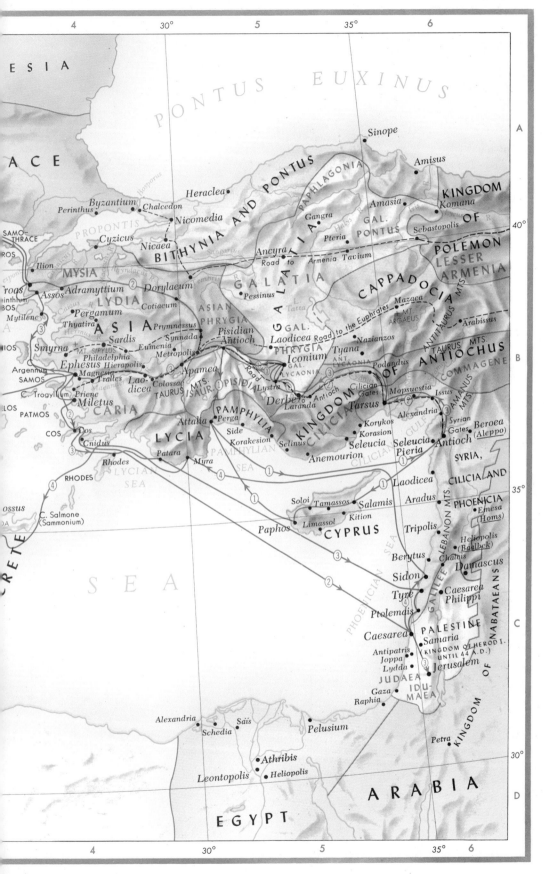

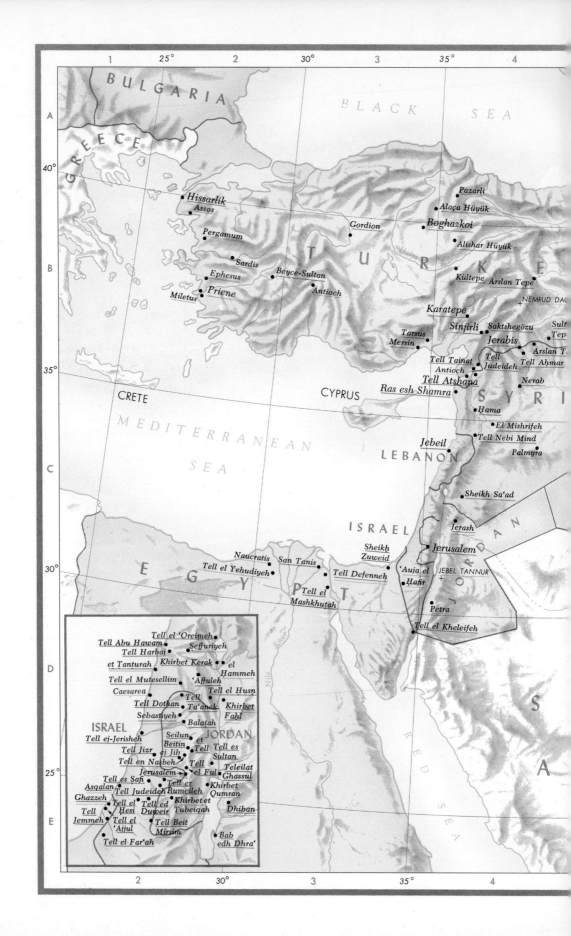

46

BULGARIA

GREECE

BLACK SEA

TURKEY

Hissarlik
Assos
Pergamum
Sardis
Ephesus
Priene
Miletus
Beyce-Sultan
Antioch

Gordion

Pazarli
Alaça Hüyük
Boghazkoi
Alishar Hüyük
Kültepe
Arslan Tepe
NEMRUD DAĞ

Karatepe
Sinjirli
Saktshegözü
Sult
Tep
Tarsus
Mersin
Jerabis
Arslan T
Tell Tainat
Antioch
Tell
Judeideh
Tell Ahmar
Tell Atshana
Ras esh Shamra
Nerab
SYRI
Ḥama

CRETE

CYPRUS

MEDITERRANEAN SEA

El Mishrifeh
Tell Nebi Mind
Palmyra
LEBANON

Sheikh Sa'ad

Jerash
JORDAN
Jerusalem
JEBEL TANNUR
+

ISRAEL

Naucratis
San Tanis
Tell el Yehudiyeh
Sheikh
Zuweid
Tell Defenneh
'Auja el
Ḥafir

EGYPT

Tell el
Mashkhutah

Petra

Tell el Kheleifeh

River Nile

S
A

RED SEA

Tell el 'Oreimeh
Tell Abu Hawam
Seffuriyeh
Tell Harbaj
et Tanturah
Khirbet Kerak
el
Ḥammeh
Tell el Mutesellim
'Affuleh
Caesarea
Tell el Husn
Tell
Ta'anek
Tell Dothan
Khirbet
Fahl
Sebastiyeh
Balatah
ISRAEL
Seilun
et
JORDAN
Tell
Tell es
Sultan
Beitin
Tell ej-Jerisheh
ej Jib
Tell Jizr
Teleilat
Ghassul
Tell en Nasbeh
Tell
el Ful
Jerusalem
Tell es Safi
Khirbet
Qumran
Tell er
Asqalan
Rumeileh
Tell Judeideh
Ghazzeh
Khirbet et
Tell el
Tell ed
Tubeiqah
Dhiban
Ḥesi
Duweir
Tell
Tell el
Jemmeh
'Ajjul
Tell Beit
Mirsim
Bab
edh Dhra'
Tell el Far'ah

MAP XXI

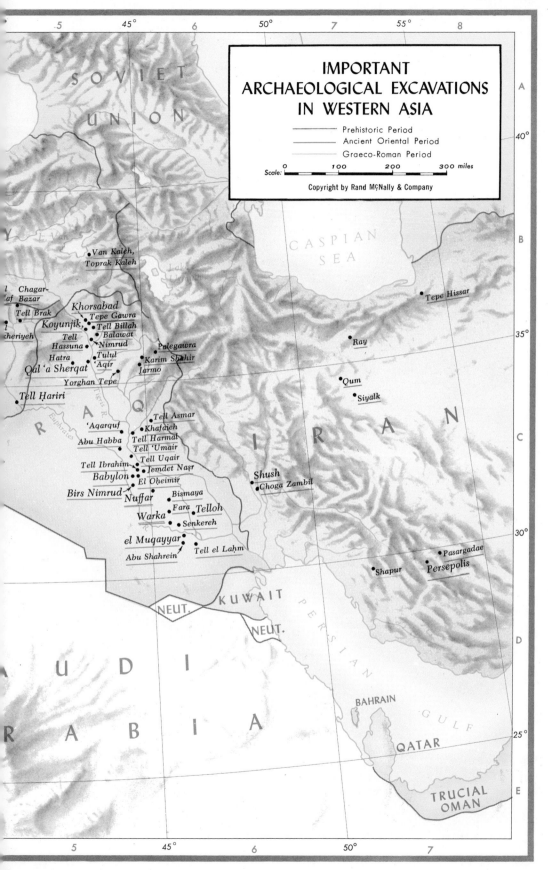

IMPORTANT ARCHAEOLOGICAL EXCAVATIONS IN WESTERN ASIA

— Prehistoric Period
— Ancient Oriental Period
— Graeco-Roman Period

Scale: 0   100   200   300 miles

Copyright by Rand McNally & Company

SOVIET UNION

CASPIAN SEA

Van Kaleh, Toprak Kaleh

Tepe Hissar

Chagar Bazar
Tell Brak
Khorsabad
Tepe Gawra
Koyunjik
Tell Billah
Tell Hassuna
Balawat
Nimrud
Hatra
Tulul
'Aqir
Qal 'a Sherqat
Karim Shahir
Jarmo
Palegawra
Yorghan Tepe
Tell Hariri

Ray

Qum
Siyalk

I R A Q

E U P H R A T E S

Tigris R.

Tell Asmar
'Aqarquf
Khafajeh
Abu Habba
Tell Harmal
Tell 'Umair
Tell Uqair
Tell Ibrahim
Jemdet Nasr
Babylon
El Oheimir
Birs Nimrud
Nuffar
Bismaya
Fara
Telloh
Warka
Senkereh
el Muqayyar
Abu Shahrein
Tell el Lahm

I R A N

Shush
Choga Zambil

Pasargadae
Shapur
Persepolis

KUWAIT
NEUT.
NEUT.

S A U D I   A R A B I A

PERSIAN GULF

BAHRAIN

QATAR

TRUCIAL OMAN

47

MAP XXII

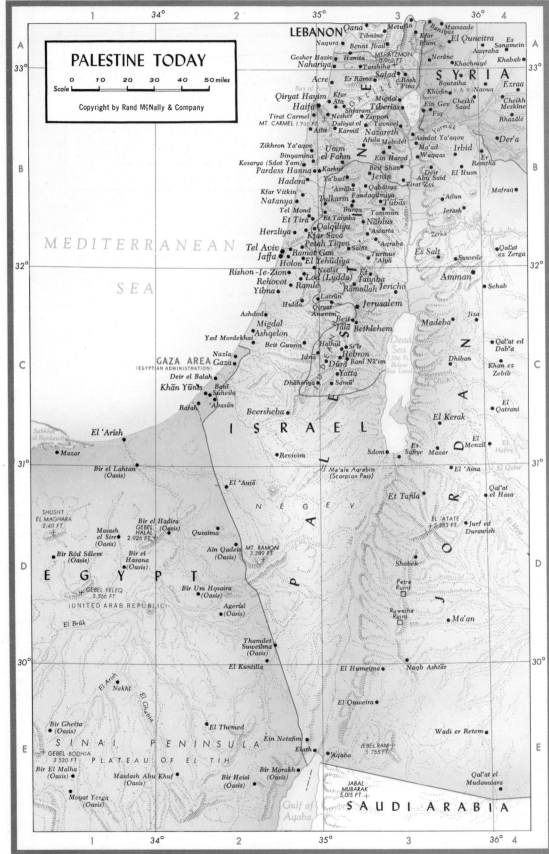

PALESTINE TODAY

Scale 0 10 20 30 40 50 miles

Copyright by Rand McNally & Company

The Ancient
Hebrew Tradition

In Gen. 1-11 we have the stories of early mankind, leading over to the migration of the ancestor of the Hebrew people, Abraham, to the Promised Land. His descendants went to Egypt in time of famine, and when a pharaoh arose "who knew not Joseph" the Hebrews were enslaved. The drawing above, showing a charioteer from the time of Seti I or Ramses II riding to the attack, with a pyramid and four bricks from an Egyptian relief alongside, excellently symbolizes this age of the oppression.

Ramses II (1301-1234 B.C.) built a city called Raamses, probably on the site of earlier Avaris and later Tanis (Biblical Zoan). Unless the mention of it by this name is an anachronism in Ex. 1:11 we are forced to consider him the Pharaoh of the oppression. Led by Moses, who had received a revelation from God at a sacred mountain, Sinai or Horeb, the Hebrews escaped into Asia and went to this same mountain, where they received laws and were sworn to a covenant relation with God.

On Color Map V various theories as to the route of the Exodus and Desert Wanderings are set forth. The traditional theory, going back to the early Church, favors the southern route to the granite mountains of the Sinaitic peninsula. The theory of a Midianite Horeb-Sinai suggests a journey via the Moslem pilgrim route to the Gulf of Aqabah, and thence southward. The Biblical references to Migdol and Baal-zephon and the quail incident (Num. 11:31), however, all point to the Mediterranean coastal area, and hence suggest a northern route. Kadesh-barnea was an important place of sojourn for the Hebrews, and by that route the migrating people would have made it their immediate objective (cf. Judg. 11:16). Under the northern theory it is attractive to assume that only a delegation went from Kadesh to the Holy Mount. From Kadesh the Hebrews went to Mt. Hor and Ezion-geber, and from there around Edom either on the east or on the west, ultimately reaching Mt. Nebo and the plains of Moab.

49

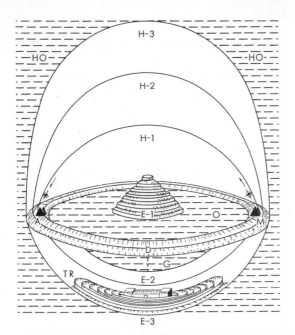

8. BABYLONIAN WORLD VIEW
(after Meissner)

E-1	Earth (Upper World)	A	Mountains of Going in of
E-2 E-3	Earth (Nether-World)		the Sun
H-1 H-2 H-3	Heavens	M	Mountains of Going forth
HO	Heavenly Ocean		of the Sun
O	Terrestrial Ocean	D	Embankment
G	Bottom of Ocean	T R	Nether-world palace and
			its seven walls

8. The Babylonian cosmology influenced that of other peoples. In Gen. 1 some ideas are much like this. The dry land emerges out of the water, and there are waters under the earth and also above the firmament. The Biblical story, however, does not mention the three stages of heaven (but cf. 2 Cor. 12:2), or the stages beneath the earth, where lay the nether-world (Heb. *Sheol*), nor the embankment, or the mountains of the sun.

9.　　BRITISH MUSEUM

9. Nimrod, legendary founder of the eastern empire (Gen. 10:8-12), was "a mighty hunter before the Lord." Assyria is called "the land of Nimrod" in Mic. 5:5. Its kings were great hunters. Here Ashurbanipal (c. 650 B.C.) honors his God after a lion hunt by pouring a libation before altar and incense stand.

10. This early Babylonian view of the world is interesting for comparison with the Hebrew world map of Gen. 2:10-14. The earth is the inner circle, while around it flows "the bitter [salt] river." The horn extending toward the Euphrates is a canal. A few cities, four in each half-circle, are indicated. The cities of Asshur and Der are named on the right, but the Tigris River is not shown.

50

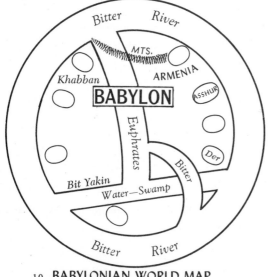

10. BABYLONIAN WORLD MAP

11. MATSON PHOTO SERVICE

11. The story of the Tower of Babel (Gen. 11) is best illustrated by what remains of the great temple tower of Ur, the best preserved one in Babylonia. These towers were of brick with a number of receding stages. That of Babylon was called in old Sumerian *E-temen-an-ki,* "House of the Foundation of Heaven and Earth." It stood in the temple called *E-sag-ila,* "House that Lifts Up the Head" (cf. Gen. 11:4). For location *see 42.*

12. Hammurabi, king of Babylon and lawgiver is of great interest, especially if he be the Amraphel king of Shinar (Babylonia) of Gen. 14. He actually was under Elam's sovereignty in his early years, as is presupposed of Amraphel. He subdued the city of Larsa, chief Elamite tributary, ruling Babylonia. By next destroying Mari, the Amorite city on the Middle Euphrates, he established the greatness of Babylon.

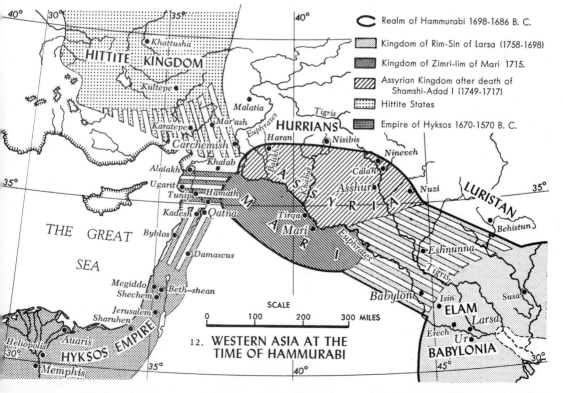

Realm of Hammurabi 1698-1686 B. C.

Kingdom of Rim-Sin of Larsa (1758-1698)

Kingdom of Zimri-lim of Mari 1715.

Assyrian Kingdom after death of Shamshi-Adad I (1749-1717)

Hittite States

Empire of Hyksos 1670-1570 B. C.

SCALE

0   100   200   300 MILES

12. WESTERN ASIA AT THE TIME OF HAMMURABI

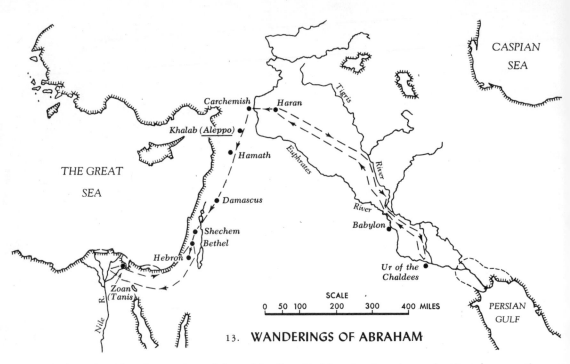

13. **WANDERINGS OF ABRAHAM**

13. Abraham is said to have migrated from Ur of the Chaldees. However, the family names Serug, Terah, Nahor, Haran point to Mesopotamia as land of origin. Furthermore Abraham has flocks, and thus is a nomad or seminomad. The Bedouin of Mesopotamia go down the Tigris in the winter, ranging as far as the Shaṭṭ el Hai (Color Map XI-C6) near Ur. Perhaps Abraham's family did the same thing. The route from Haran to the Promised Land is not described in the Bible, but one via Carchemish, Aleppo, Damascus is suggested.

14. The air view shows the French excavations at Mari, and in the distance the Euphrates, which once ran close to the city. Zimri-lim, last king of Mari, had a famous palace with 300 rooms, covering 6 acres. Some of these were decorated with mural paintings in beautiful colors. The archives have shed rich light on Mesopotamian history. The letters of Shamshi-Adad I, king of Assyria, to his son who was governor of Mari, are especially revealing. Mari had again become powerful after the death of Shamshi-Adad I.

14. INSTITUT FRANCAIS D'ARCHÉOLOGIE. BEYROUTH. LIBAN

15. Abraham, the servant he sent back to Haran (Gen. 24), and Jacob all traveled past Aleppo, for the route via Palmyra to the Euphrates was not in use then. The mound of the ancient city is clearly visible, but unfortunately cannot be excavated. In the early second millennium Khalab (or Khalpa), as the city was called, was the capital of the kingdom of Yamkhad. An intelligence report sent to Zimri-lim of Mari states that "twenty kings follow Yarim-lim of Yamkhad." It ranks him with the kings of Babylon and of Larsa.

16. Hebron is an important place in Patriarchal history. Here Abraham bought the cave of Machpelah for a tomb (Gen. 23). Here not only he but Isaac and Jacob are said to have been buried. This cave no doubt is the one now situated in the Haram, or sacred enclosure. The traditional site of Mamre is at Ramet el Khalil, "the Height of the Friend." The new Genesis Apocryphon from Qumran already presupposes this localization when it describes it as "east of the north of Hebron." Ancient Hebron probably lay on the hill west of the tomb of the patriarchs.

17. Gen. 14 reports an invasion of Palestine in the time of Abraham. The world-historical background is obscure, but the geography of the campaign is clear. The invaders came down through Transjordan, subduing 1) the Bronze Age cities Ashtaroth, Karnaim, and Ham; 2) Shaveh-kiriathaim, or better "the vale" of Kiriathaim, a city of Moab; 3) the pre-Edomite inhabitants of Mt. Seir as far as El Paran (otherwise Elath), on the Gulf of Aqabah. Thence they went to Kadesh, here called En Mishpat, "Well of Judgment," and Hazazontamar near En-gedi, and then to the vale of Siddim,

15. INSTITUT FRANCAIS D'ARCHÉOLOGIE, BEYROUTH, LIBAN

where they battled the kinglets of Sodom, etc. Abraham pursued them to Dan and after defeating them there followed them to Hobah north of Damascus. The new Genesis Apocryphon from Qumran has Helbon (cf. Ezek. 27:18) for Hobah.

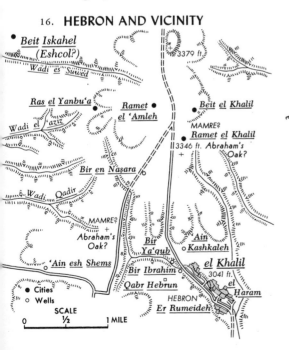

16. **HEBRON AND VICINITY**

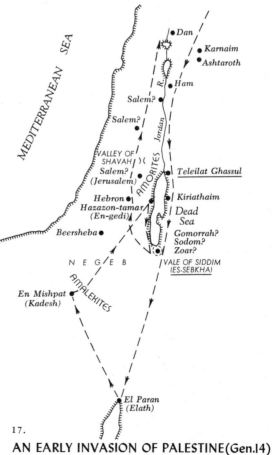

17.

AN EARLY INVASION OF PALESTINE (Gen. 14)

53

18. Israel regarded Jacob as its more immediate "ancestor." His name echoes that of a king of the Hyksos—the Asiatics who ruled Egypt 1670-1570 B.C. Esau, Jacob's brother, was considered ancestor of the Edomites. The stories about them reflect the foibles and fates of both peoples. Archaeology has shown that Edom was virtually without inhabited cities from 1900-1300 B.C. Jacob fled before Esau to his relatives in Mesopotamia. That region was invaded by a new population, the Aramaeans, from 1300-1100 B.C. Laban the Aramaean became Jacob's father-in-law. When Jacob went back to Palestine, he was pursued by Laban, and a boundary treaty was made between Hebrew and Aramaean at or near Gilead (Gen. 31:21, 44f.). Via Mahanaim and Penuel, where he received the name "Israel," Jacob went to Shechem.

19. Shechem was the natural center of Palestine. In the Amarna age (c. 1400 B.C.) an important kingdom flourished here. Old Shechem lay at Tell Balaṭah. German diggings from 1913 on have been succeeded by American ones since 1957. Memories of Abraham, Jacob, Joseph, Joshua, and Abimelech —to speak only of early Hebrew story—are associated with this place.

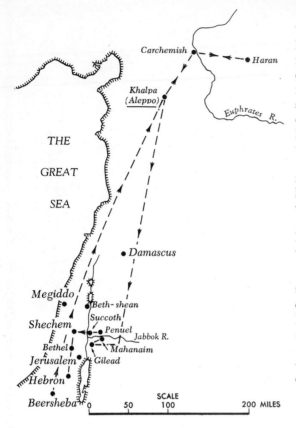

THE

GREAT

SEA

18. **WANDERINGS OF JACOB**

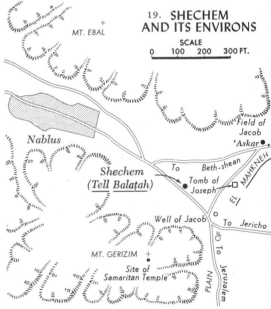

19. **SHECHEM AND ITS ENVIRONS**

20. The traditional Mt. Sinai is the Jebel Mūsa. It seems probable that this eminence, the highest point of the range, was always the holiest part. The Rās Ṣafṣafeh at the north end which has been much favored as the scene of the lawgiving, has enjoyed consideration chiefly because there is more room at its foot for large encampments. On this photo one looks from Jebel Mūsa toward the region in which Kadesh lay. If Deut. 1:2 calls it an 11-day journey from Horeb to Kadesh that corresponds quite well to reality.

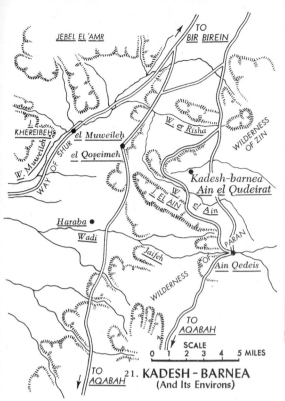

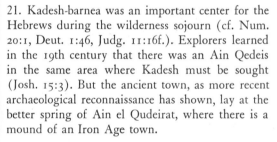

21. **KADESH - BARNEA**
(And Its Environs)

22.   MATSON PHOTO SERVICE

21. Kadesh-barnea was an important center for the Hebrews during the wilderness sojourn (cf. Num. 20:1, Deut. 1:46, Judg. 11:16f.). Explorers learned in the 19th century that there was an Ain Qedeis in the same area where Kadesh must be sought (Josh. 15:3). But the ancient town, as more recent archaeological reconnaissance has shown, lay at the better spring of Ain el Qudeirat, where there is a mound of an Iron Age town.

22. As a first step in the departure from Kadesh, a journey to Mt. Hor on the boundary of Edom is related (Num. 20:22-29, 33:37). Here Aaron, the brother of Moses, died. Josephus puts the mountain at Petra. Not far from that capital of the ancient

Nabataeans is a height called *Jebel Hārūn,* the "Prophet Aaron" (Color Map V-B7). His supposed tomb is a rebuilt Christian church of c. A.D. 550.

23. From Kadesh the Israelites set out by the way to the Red Sea (the Gulf of Aqabah) to go around the land of Edom (Num. 21:4, cf. Judg. 11:17-18). One could well imagine them desiring to pass through Edom itself from the south. The photo shows the view from the ancient forts guarding the ascent into Edom, the Neqb Shtar (Color Map V-B7). One is looking in the direction of Midian proper, where some scholars locate the mountain of God (V-D6). A different version of the events, perhaps representing another group, took Israel up through the Arabah-rift into Moab. Here some names like Oboth, Punon, and Iye-Abarim can be localized (V-B7).

23.   COURTESY NELSON GLUECK

55

The
Promised Land

AFTER THE DEATH of Moses, the Hebrews under Joshua crossed the Jordan and after a stop at Gilgal captured Jericho. Recent excavations have shown this to be one of earth's oldest cities, with remains going back to 6000 B.C.

The Conquest of Ai near Bethel struck a blow piercing into the upland regions. The Covenant with Gibeon, "a great city, like one of the royal cities," brought the invaders the rule of a large enclave. A victory of Joshua over an alliance of kings in a battle near Gibeon extended Hebrew control westward to the coastal plain.

In the north a victory was won by the waters of Merom (near Safed) over a coalition headed by Hazor, near Lake Semechonitis. At Shechem Joshua gave his farewell address.

The grim era of conquest is well symbolized in the drawing above, showing a Canaanite fortress and Canaanite suppliants from Egyptian reliefs, with a spearhead (drawn from one of this period found at

Megiddo) leveled in their direction.

The ensuing century reveals the individual tribes concerned with their own territories. Co-operative action, however, was undertaken in common peril. Such was the case in the battle of Taanach "by the waters of Megiddo" in the Plain of Esdraelon, as reported in story and song (Judg. 4–5). Little co-operation was shown at the time of the Midianite invasion which was mastered by the Manassite Gideon of Ophrah. His son Abimelech first ruled and then destroyed Shechem (Judg. 9). The Transjordanian tribes produced a hero named Jephthah (of Mizpeh or Gilead) in the face of peril from the Ammonites. The Danites living on the edge of the Philistine country had a hero named Samson, who performed great exploits. But in the end they were forced to migrate to a new home at the headwaters of the Jordan where they seized Laish (the "lion-city"), which they renamed Dan. Intertribal war occurred, too, and Benjamin was gravely weakened in the one reported.

24.   MATSON PHOTO SERVICE

24. The photo was taken from a point close to the Qumran and Scrolls' caves areas (*see* 1). We are thus looking across the head of the Dead Sea to the opposite eastern side, from a point a little farther south. Mt. Nebo, on which Moses stood to view the Promised Land (*see* 2) is but a promontory of high tableland. It lies to the right of the break in the range visible on the left. The whole upper tier of the slope country was called Abarim in the Old Testament. Whether Pisgah is a section of it that included Mt. Nebo, or the lower more forward eminence (Ras Ṣiyaghah) cannot be decided. East of the head of the Dead Sea, up a stream valley, was Beth-jeshimoth. Israel lay encamped from here to Abel-shittim (Num. 33:49), a few miles to the north. This whole district was called "the plains of Moab." Beyond the right edge of the picture lies the valley of the Arnon, of which Jephthah said "the Arnon is the (northern!) boundary of Moab" (Judg. 11:18).

25.   MATSON PHOTO SERVICE

25. The crossing of the Jordan is the momentous prelude to the conquest of Canaan. It is said to have taken place at freshet time, when the stream was not fordable. But the impossible became possible for Israel through a stoppage of the stream many miles above "at Adam, the city that is beside Zarethan" (Josh. 3:16). The flow of the river has been blocked a number of times in recorded history —most recently in 1927, when the fall of a high cliff dammed the stream for 21 hours. This took place in the very area mentioned in the Bible. The photo shows a stretch of river where such a thing could well happen, when the water undermines the rock at a bend. In the background are the mountains of Judah.

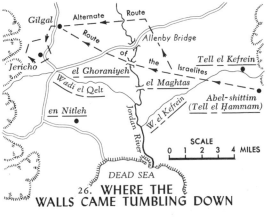

26. WHERE THE WALLS CAME TUMBLING DOWN

57

26. The Israelites came next to Gilgal and there held religious rites. Long sought southeast of Jericho, it now seems more probable Gilgal lay northeast. This indicates a more northerly crossing of the river than at the Hajleh ford. Jericho was then taken. The city, in which excavations have been conducted since 1907, first by German, then by British archaeologists, has thus far produced only Early and Middle Bronze Age remains for the historical period. At the time of the conquest it may not have been as strong as in earlier days.

27.   MATSON PHOTO SERVICE

of a number of kingdoms. The photo shows the huge mound of Tell el Qedah, which covers 150 acres and fits all the requirements for Hazor's location (*see* Color Map VI-B4). A Hebrew University expedition has been carrying on excavations there. The thirteenth city on the site was the one of Joshua's time. It was destroyed in the 13th century B.C.—presumably by Joshua. The city is providing rich illustration of Canaanite religion and culture.

28.   MATSON PHOTO SERVICE

27. From Jericho the Israelites captured Ai (*see* 30), a city in which French excavations were conducted in 1933-34. The next great battle was that at Gibeon with a coalition of kings that sought to punish Gibeon for making an alliance with Joshua. That Gibeon lay at ej Jib has been established by the recent American excavations (since 1956), in which jar handles inscribed with the ancient name were found. Another discovery was that of the pool of Gibeon, with 42 steps leading down and a guard-rail cut from solid rock. Various events took place here (2 Sam. 2:13, Jer. 41:12). Part of ancient Gibeon is occupied by a town and so inaccessible to excavation.

28. A victory of Joshua over Hazor and capture of the city are said to have clinched control of northern Palestine for Israel (Josh. 11:10f.). It was the head

29. The most important event recorded in Judges is the battle of Taanach "by the waters of Megiddo." A coalition of tribes here defeated Sisera, king of Harosheth, a dependency of Hazor. Barak assembled his forces on Mt. Tabor. The photo looks down on the battlefield from the spur of Mt. Carmel. The tell of ancient Megiddo, a mound of 15 acres, is visible on the right. German digging was carried on here in 1903. Large scale excavations were conducted by American expeditions from 1924 on. The Megiddo Ivories (*see* 31) and Solomon's stables were important finds. Megiddo may have been uninhabited at the time of Barak.

29.   MATSON PHOTO SERVICE

The Great Kings

THE GLAMOROUS FIGURES of Israel's history are Saul, David, and Solomon. Saul of Gibeah in Benjamin first achieved a rule of all Israel and Judah. He delivered the Hebrews of Jabesh in Gilead from the Ammonites, defeated the Philistine invaders, and crushed the Amalekites in the extreme south. But he perished on Mt. Gilboa in a new war with the Philistines. His ex-harpist and son-in-law David of Bethlehem, whom he had jealously persecuted, set up an independent kingdom of Judah at Hebron. The Benjaminite monarchy, now ruled from Mahanaim, collapsed with the death of Ishbosheth (Eshbaal), and the northern tribes offered David the crown. By capturing Jerusalem from the Canaanites he found a more suitable capital.

David's achievements were great. He besieged and captured Rabbath Ammon (today Amman, capital of the kingdom of Jordan), conquered Moab and Edom, decisively defeated the Philistines, and expanded his power into Syria, where he held Damascus.

The realm continued to flourish and to attain a higher culture under Solomon. The drawing above shows a Phoenician ship and logs from Assyrian reliefs and a cedar tree from a Persepolis relief as symbols of the building activity of this era.

Solomon's queen was a daughter of Pharaoh, and the latter captured the city of Gezer and gave it to her for a dowry. Solomon organized the kingdom on a more modern basis. He exercised influence in Syria, and with the aid of Tyre sent ships to Ophir (probably on the African Coast). He developed Ezion-geber on the Gulf of Aqabah as a seaport for this trade and smelting-place for the copper mined in the Arabah-rift north of Aqabah. That he allowed his foreign wives to introduce pagan cults was the chief blot on his record. His fame for wisdom was such that it drew a visit of the queen of distant Sheba in what is now Saudi Arabia.

59

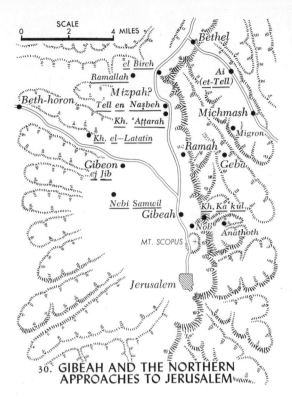

SCALE
0   2   4 MILES

30. GIBEAH AND THE NORTHERN
APPROACHES TO JERUSALEM

north to Shechem and beyond, and the road to the left headed for the Plain of Sharon and the coast. American excavations in 1922-23 uncovered the earliest datable Israelite fortification yet found, for the pottery can be assigned to 1020-1000 B.C., the time of Saul. Ramah here is not the Ramah of Samuel, but that of 1 Kings 15:47. At Michmash occurred Jonathan's exploit (1 Sam. 14). At Nob David obtained shewbread and Goliath's sword (1 Sam. 21). Jerusalem was still a Canaanite possession, though no doubt tributary like Gibeon.

30. The Gibeah of Benjamin, 3½ miles north of Jerusalem, the capital of the first Hebrew Kingdom embracing both Judah and Israel, commanded an important fork in the roads. The straight road went

31. In the excavations at Megiddo fine ivory carvings, used as inlays on furniture, were found. This remarkable one (c. 1200 B.C.) may have decorated a king's throne. The ruler, sitting on a throne ornamented with a winged, human-headed creature, may have been one of those who held in check the men of Israel's tribe of Manasseh (Judg. 1:27). A musician plays before him, as David played before Saul. Solomon later had such a stylish ivory throne (1 Kings 10:18).

32. When Saul and Jonathan perished in the battle of Mt. Gilboa, the Philistines hung their bodies on the gates of Beth-shean, which lay on this mound excavated by Americans in 1921-33. It was an important fortress of Egypt in the 14th-12th centuries B.C., and inscribed stelas of Pharaoh Seti I were found here. In Hellenistic Roman times the place was known as Scythopolis.

31.   THE ORIENTAL INSTITUTE, UNIVERSITY OF CHICAGO

32.   MATSON PHOTO SERVICE

33.   INSTITUT FRANCAIS D'ARCHÉOLOGIE, BEYROUTH, LIBAN

33. When David captured the fortress of Jerusalem, he laid the foundation for a powerful monarchy. It was left to Solomon to build the temple, a modern palace, and other royal buildings. With the help of Hiram, king of Tyre, Solomon obtained both the precious cedar wood and skilled artisans. Tyre, originally an impregnable island city, was founded from Sidon in 1195 B.C. But it outstripped its parent. A vivid picture of its role in the 6th century is given in Ezek. 27. Alexander the Great captured it in 332 B.C. by building a mole out to it. This mole, through sanding up, has become an isthmus.

34. The reconstruction below of Solomon's acropolis uses ground plans of contemporary, corresponding structures for the Hall of the Throne and Hall of Pillars. The temple sketch shows a profile of the "house" or sanctum that stood within the temple court, and the steps of the inner sanctuary leading up to where the Ark of the Covenant reposed. For the temple at the time of Christ, see 58.

35. In the time of the first kings, Jerusalem occupied about 11 acres on a ridge 40 yards wide. In the center of this photo lies the temple quadrangle constructed by Herod. To the left of it a depression runs down—the Tyropoeon Valley. The deep valley on the right, or east, is the Kidron Valley, adjacent to which is the Mt. of Olives (see 59). Ancient Jerusalem was perhaps confined to the ridge south of the temple (see Color Maps XVII, XVIII). Below, on the right, lay the Gihon Spring, where the kings were anointed. Through the ridge was cut the Siloam tunnel leading the Gihon waters to the pool of Siloam on the west side. The area once occupied by the palace of Solomon doubtless lies buried under the southern part of the great quadrangle. Later the city grew larger and took in the northern part of the western hill. In the time of Christ it may have occupied the whole western hill. In Christian annals Sion is the western hill. The Jews themselves had come to believe mistakenly that the City of David had lain here.

35.   MATSON PHOTO SERVICE

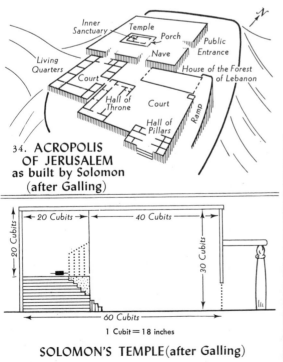

Inner Sanctuary   Temple   Porch   Public Entrance

Nave

Living Quarters

House of the Forest of Lebanon

Court

Hall of Throne   Court

Hall of Pillars

Ramp

N

34. ACROPOLIS OF JERUSALEM as built by Solomon (after Galling)

20 Cubits

20 Cubits   40 Cubits

30 Cubits

60 Cubits

1 Cubit = 18 inches

SOLOMON'S TEMPLE (after Galling)

The Divided Kingdom

UNDER SOLOMON's SON Rehoboam Israel seceded from Judah. Jeroboam I of Israel made Shechem his capital, but we soon find him and his successors at Tirzah (1 Kings 14:17). At this time occurred the Palestinian campaign of Pharaoh Shishak, who "took away everything" from Jerusalem. Asa of Judah and Baasha of Israel carried on border strife, and the former appealed for help to Benhadad of Aram (Damascus was Aram's capital) who then invaded Israel.

The outstanding rulers of Israel were Omri and Ahab. The former built the new capital Samaria. Ahab fell in battle with the Aramaeans. His son Jehoram and the visiting Ahaziah of Judah were both slain by the usurper Jehu. In Judah, Athaliah, mother of Ahaziah but kin to Ahab, seized the reins until a revolution set up an infant son of Ahaziah.

Israel suffered greatly at the hands of Aram, and Judah too became tributary. The former state waxed strong again under Joash and Jeroboam II. Joash defeated Amaziah of Judah, but Azariah of Judah prospered.

Under Tiglathpileser III, Assyria now took a hand in the west. Menahem of Israel paid tribute. When another usurper, Pekah, invaded Judah with Rezin of Aram, King Ahaz put himself under the protection of the Assyrians. Tiglathpileser fell upon Israel and annexed important districts. Damascus was destroyed by him in 732 B.C., Samaria by Sargon in 721. The Israelites were carried off to captivity in northern regions.

Judah under King Hezekiah resisted the Assyrians, and suffered a destructive invasion at the hands of Sennacherib in 701 B.C. Manasseh was a loyal Assyrian retainer. The decline of Assyria made possible a Judaean expansion under Josiah, but he perished in opposing Pharaoh Necho when the latter marched to the Euphrates to aid the king of Assyria. After Assyria's fall Nebuchadnezzar became Judah's overlord. Judah rebelled but surrendered in 597; its king Jehoiachin and the aristocracy were deported. The new ruler, Zedekiah, rebelled in 586 B.C. Jerusalem was destroyed and the remaining population deported to Babylonia.

The design above shows a winged Assyrian figure with zodiacal symbols of the Moon and Venus-star, taken from Assyrian reliefs, and a lion from one of the cities of Israel's captivity, Gozan, now Tell Halaf in Mesopotamia.

36. One of the significant events of the history of Israel was the founding of the Omri Dynasty. "House of Omri" was used as a term for Israel by the Assyrians long after there were no rulers of that house. Omri was a soldier and was besieging the Philistine-held city Gibbethon when Zimri murdered king Elah, son of Baasha, at Tirzah. Departing from Gibbethon, Omri swiftly besieged and destroyed Tirzah, and usurped the throne. A later siege of Gibbethon is shown on this sculpture from the palace of the Assyrian king, Sargon II. It is portrayed as perched on a wooded hill.

37. The Stela of King Ashurnaṣirpal of Assyria was discovered in recent British excavations at Calah (Gen. 10:11), today Nimrud. It shows king Ashurnaṣirpal, and was erected at the entrance to his palace. Symbols of the gods are shown above— Moon, winged solar disk, Venus-star, and others. The inscription mentions a great celebration held at the dedication of his palace, when he feasted the entire population of 69,574 persons for 10 days, a marvelous confirmation for the possibility of Ahasuerus' seven-day banquet for all the people of Susa or Shushan (Esther 1:5).

36.   AFTER BOTTA AND FLANDIN

sieged in Samaria by his rival (1 Kings 20). Another siege took place under a successor (2 Kings 6:24f.). But the most desperate was the last, when Samaria was besieged for three years by Shalmaneser IV (2 Kings 17:5) and his successor Sargon II, who, according to his own report, was the actual destroyer. New colonists were settled here in place of the deported inhabitants (2 Kings 17:24). Important excavations have been conducted at Samaria since 1901 by American and British archaeologists. The palaces of Omri and Ahab and inscribed sherds (ostraca) of the early 8th century B.C. were found. (On the later history, see 60.)

37.   BRITISH SCHOOL OF ARCHAEOLOGY IN IRAQ

38.   MATSON PHOTO SERVICE

38. The noble hill of Samaria was a suitable site for the capital of a kingdom. One can imagine Israel's kings, amid public acclaim, setting forth from here on their campaigns. One of these, only reported in Assyrian inscriptions, was Ahab's participation in a coalition defeated at Qarqar in Syria by Shalmaneser III in 853 B.C. Ahab furnished a contingent of 2,000 chariots and 10,000 men. While allied here with the king of Aram, he carried on war with him at other times, and was even be-

39.   BRITISH MUSEUM

39. Soon after Jehu gained the throne, he had to pay tribute to the Assyrian king Shalmaneser III (842 B.C.) He is shown here prostrating himself before that ruler. The scene is from the Black Obelisk found long ago at Calah. The incident of this tribute, like that of the battle of Qarqar, is not reported in the Book of Kings. The invasion of Israel by Tiglathpileser III in 733 B.C. and Sennacherib's invasion of Judah in 701 B.C. are reported by both Hebrews and Assyrians.

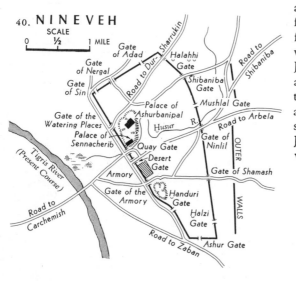

40. **N I N E V E H**

40. Nineveh is the most important city of Assyria, having succeeded Asshur as the capital. British excavations a century ago had spectacular success here. Palaces of Sennacherib and Ashurbanipal were unearthed. Recent digs had no such results. The plan shows the city and its gates and the site of the two palaces. The river Ḫusur is worth noting. It is still called "Choser" today. According to Greek reports a freshet of this river caused a stretch of the wall to collapse and enabled the enemy to rush in.

The fate of the city was sealed by the joint action of Kyaxares, king of Media, and Nabopolassar of Babylon. They took the city in 612 B.C. The prophet Nahum followed these events closely. A last stand of the Assyrians was made at Haran, which fell in 606 B.C.

41. Great light was shed on the events connected with the fall of Nineveh by a Babylonian Chronicle published in 1923. A further Chronicle text published in 1956 and shown here has given us new and authentic information about the happenings from 608-595 B.C. It reports Nebuchadnezzar's defeat of Pharaoh Necho at Carchemish in 605 B.C., with pursuit and total annihilation of his forces (cf. Jer. 46). It records Nebuchadnezzar's succession and his conquest of Palestine, so vividly reflected in the prophecy of Habakkuk. It relates a campaign against Egypt in 601 B.C., which failed, and the siege and first capture of "the city of Juda," i.e. Jerusalem, on March 16, 597 B.C. (exact date previously unknown).

41.   BRITISH MUSEUM

Babylon
to Jerusalem

THE DAYS of the Neo-Babylonian kingdom were numbered. King Nabonidus incurred the enmity of the priesthood of Babylon, and sought safety in Tema in Arabia, entrusting his son Belshazzar with governing. Cyrus, king of the half-nomadic Persians, conquered Media in 550 B.C. and Lydia in 546. He turned against mighty Babylon in 539. Nabonidus was on hand, but treason rendered his defense futile.

Under Cyrus the Jews were permitted to return to Judaea. At the time of Darius I, urged on by the prophets Haggai and Zechariah, they began to rebuild the temple. In 445 B.C. Nehemiah, a Jew, cupbearer of King Artaxerxes I, went from Susa to Jerusalem and managed to get its walls rebuilt in spite of opposition by the foreign aristocracy at Samaria. Ezra the Scribe came from Babylonia and brought the Jews "the Law of the God of Heaven." It is possible that he came under Artaxerxes II in 398 B.C. rather than under Artaxerxes I (in 458 B.C.).

The design shown above pictures a Persian king and a procession of his spearmen from a Persepolis relief, and the cuneiform inscription is from a silver tablet from a foundation deposit at that capital, where Nehemiah, too, will often have attended his sovereign. It symbolizes the era in which Judaism began to develop under the protection of the King of kings.

The last high priest mentioned in Neh. 12:11 is Jaddua. According to Josephus he was still in office at the coming of Alexander the Great, 332 B.C. The Ptolemies of Egypt controlled Palestine from 320-198 B.C. After that it belonged to the Seleucid kings ruling at Antioch in Syria. The policy of Antiochus Epiphanes IV, who wanted to force his religion and culture on the Jews brought about the Maccabean uprising in 167 B.C. Out of that gradually came a Maccabean state, which under Alexander Jannaeus ruled all Palestine. Both the weakened Seleucid monarchy and the Maccabean kingdom collapsed when Pompey appeared on the scene in 63 B.C. Roman troops stormed the temple.

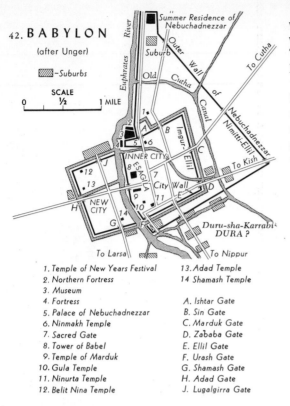

42. BABYLON
(after Unger)

▨ – Suburbs

SCALE
0   ½   1 MILE

1. Temple of New Years Festival
2. Northern Fortress
3. Museum
4. Fortress
5. Palace of Nebuchadnezzar
6. Ninmakh Temple
7. Sacred Gate
8. Tower of Babel
9. Temple of Marduk
10. Gula Temple
11. Ninurta Temple
12. Belit Nina Temple
13. Adad Temple
14 Shamash Temple

A. Ishtar Gate
B. Sin Gate
C. Marduk Gate
D. Zababa Gate
E. Ellil Gate
F. Urash Gate
G. Shamash Gate
H. Adad Gate
J. Lugalgirra Gate

with its great tower, was the temple of Marduk, whose name is vocalized Merodach in the Bible. The deity was also called Bēl, "lord," (cf. Jer. 50:2). From here the god Marduk was taken out to the "House of the New Year's Festival" (1), where the king had to "seize the hands of Marduk" and be reinstated in his office for another year. The procession then returned through the Ishtar Gate (A) and along a street lined by high walls of glazed brick and ornamented with lions, dragons, and other figures. The main defenses of the city were in the north, as were the most important palaces. In 5 lay the Palace of Nebuchadnezzar; the "hanging gardens" of the Greek writers were probably to the northeast, near the Ishtar Gate. The summer residence in the north has not been fully excavated. It is to this mound that the name *Bābil* has clung through the centuries.

43. The Palace of Nebuchadnezzar as revealed by excavations. On the south is the throne room, 56 feet wide, 173 feet long. Here, if anywhere, one must imagine the scene of Belshazzar's feast. Opposite the middle entrance in the rear wall is a niche, occupied no doubt by the royal throne. On a wall of this room appeared the ambiguous handwriting in Aramaic (Dan. 5:25) which Daniel interpreted as "numbered, numbered, weighed, and divided."

44. At Naksh-i-Rustem near Persepolis, Darius I had his tomb hewn into a cliff, and Xerxes, Artaxerxes I, and Darius II followed his example. The lower part portrays the facade of a royal palace. The

42. German excavations of 1899-1917 uncovered much of the city of Nebuchadnezzar. The Euphrates passed through it, but the important structures were all on the left bank of the river. The holy gate leading into the temple area gave the whole city its name *Bab-ili*, "Gate of God." *E-sag-ila*, "the House that Lifts Up the Head," (cf. Gen. 11:4),

43. THE PALACE OF NEBUCHADNEZZAR

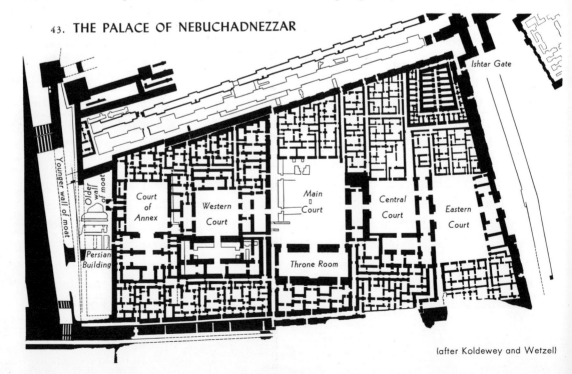

(after Koldewey and Wetzel)

44.   THE ORIENTAL INSTITUTE, UNIVERSITY OF CHICAGO

Jehovah). The first papyri found here were bought by an American visitor in 1893. Lost sight of for many years through his death, they were first published in 1953 by the editor of this book. Papyri found later were published in 1906 and 1911.

46. No name struck such dread into the heart of the Greeks as that of Xerxes, who sought to conquer their land. Greek victories excited nationalism, but it took Philip of Macedon and his son Alexander to teach the Greek states to co-operate. Alexander felt himself the agent of Greek revenge when he conquered the Persian empire and cast the torch into the palace of Xerxes. The photo shows what remains of this palace on the great terrace of Persepolis.

small building, facing the tombs of Darius I and Artaxerxes I here shown, is called "the tomb of Zoroaster," but was probably a fire-temple, in which the imperial standard was kept. Darius had obtained the throne by putting down the rebellion of the magian Gaumata, who claimed to be the brother of Cambyses at the latter's death. The great sculptures and inscriptions on the mountain of Behistun commemorate Darius' victory. He made Persepolis his capital, with Susa a close second. An American expedition excavated at Persepolis from 1931 on.

45. A large group of Jews who spoke Aramaic and wrote letters and legal documents in this language lived at the military colony on Elephantine Island (Yeb), where there was a temple of their national God. Enlisted by the Egyptians in the 6th century B.C., they served Persia after Cambyses conquered Egypt in 525 B.C. The colony probably perished soon after the year 400 B.C. when the Persians lost control of Egypt for a period. The photos show an Aramaic papyrus roll with seal and string in place. The author of the document was a functionary of the God Yahu (the short form of Yahweh,

45.   BROOKLYN MUSEUM

46.   THE ORIENTAL INSTITUTE, UNIVERSITY OF CHICAGO

The Time of Jesus

POMPEY had appointed Hyrcanus II high priest and ethnarch. The Idumaean Antipater and his sons ably assisted the latter. Julius Caesar, to whom Hyrcanus and Antipater gave valuable aid in Egypt in 48 B.C., honored both and gave the seaport Joppa back to the Jews. But soon the Parthians, who had reestablished a Persian empire, invaded Syria. With their aid Antigonus, son of Hyrcanus' rival brother, became king of Judaea.

In the year 40 B.C. the Roman Senate conferred the crown of Judaea on Antipater's son Herod. It was up to him to conquer the country. He accomplished this, and Antigonus was executed by the Romans. Herod married Mariamne, granddaughter of Hyrcanus II. When Octavius became Caesar Augustus, he entrusted Herod with kingship over all Palestine. Herod was a great builder; he rebuilt the temple magnificently and he founded the city of Caesarea on the coast north of Joppa.

The time of Augustus was a golden age of peace for the Near East. The design above showing a Roman triumphal arch, a Roman soldier and a coin of Augustus Caesar symbolizes this period.

The realm of Herod was divided between three sons. Archelaus received Judaea, Samaria, and Idumaea, and the title ethnarch; Herod Antipas got Galilee and Peraea with the title tetrarch. Philip had the same title and was given the northeastern regions. Archelaus was removed from office by Augustus in A.D. 6 and his territory put under direct Roman management by a procurator who resided at Caesarea. The fifth of these procurators was Pontius Pilate (A.D. 26-36). Jesus' ministry began in the fifteenth year of Tiberius (Luke 3:1), i.e., A.D. 27-28 or 28-29, depending on whether Luke reckoned in Western or Eastern manner. Neither the date of Jesus' birth or Crucifixion can be definitely ascertained; A.D. 30 is the most widely accepted year for the latter.

47.   MATSON PHOTO SERVICE

47. That history would repeat itself and another David would go forth from Bethlehem in the district of Ephrath(ah) was the rapturous prediction of a Judaean prophet (Mic. 5:2). Buried beyond hope of recovery is the Bethlehem of David and his remote descendant Joseph, son of Jacob. All that remains is the topography, which dictates where the town must have stood and where the fields lay, above which angels sang their *gloria in excelsis*. The most prominent building is the Church of the Nativity, one of Christendom's most ancient churches, for the nave is part of the original structure Constantine raised on this spot. It was built over a cave, believed to have been the place of the Nativity. The cave has a niche in the rock which can be construed as a manger. Justin Martyr (c. A.D. 150) already refers to this cave, and some Greek manuscripts have "cave" instead of "manger" in Luke 2:7.

up to it. Numerous buildings for guests, retainers, and servants lay at its foot. Water was led there from afar. Herod was buried in the fortress, which was apparently destroyed by Romans at the time of Hadrian, c. A.D. 135.

49. "And he went and dwelt in a city called Nazareth," says an evangelist of Joseph (Matt. 2:23). It is this city more than any other with which the name of Jesus is connected. Yet it remained hostile to Christianity as late as the 4th century A.D.: St. Paula (A.D. 386) hurried through here without stopping. By A.D. 670, however, Nazareth had two Christian churches, one where the home of Jesus had stood, and the other over the house where the angel had appeared to the Virgin Mary. But Moslem fanaticism obliterated all Christian sites in Nazareth after the defeat of the Crusaders. The holy places of today are without any continuity of tradition. One looks here toward the Plain of Esdraelon and the drop-off to it, which is implausibly connected with the "brow of the hill" of Luke 4:28. The mountain is the Jebel ed Daḥi, sometimes mistakenly called Little Hermon because of Ps. 89:12 mentioning Tabor and Hermon together, or connected with the Hill of Moreh (Judg. 7:1)

49.   ISRAEL GOVERNMENT TOURIST OFFICE

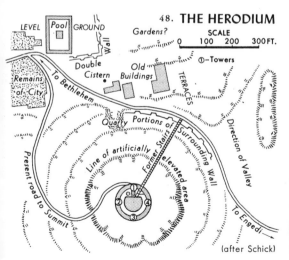

48. THE HERODIUM

SCALE

0 100 200 300 FT.

(after Schick)

48. The Herodium, a fortress built by the Herod of Matt. 2:1f., lay on the flat-topped Frank Mountain southeast of Bethlehem. Numerous round towers broke the expanse of its walls, and marble stairs led

50. The Gospels according to Mark and John begin their story with John the Baptist. He baptized at Bethabara (A.V.), or Bethany (R.S.V.) supposedly beyond the Jordan (John 1:28). In the mosaic map found on the floor of a 6th century Christian church at Madeba in Moab, however, Bethabara is put this side of the Jordan. That suggests that the name is corrupted from Beth-arabah, a town southeast of Jericho. On the other side of the river the map has "Ainon there, now Sapsaphas," rather than Bethany. Perhaps an original Beth-ainon became Bethany (Bethania) under influence of the name of the town near Jerusalem. The large oval in the mosaic is a surprisingly detailed portrayal of Christian Jerusalem. Northeast of Jericho, with its palms, is put Gilgal and the Dodekalithon (the Twelve-stone Church, cf. Josh. 4:8).

51. To the southwest of Nazareth lay Japhia (today Yāfa), in its time the more important place. Sepphoris, the capital of Galilee before Antipas built Tiberias, was destroyed by the Romans during a rebellion after the death of Herod in 4 B.C. Its inhabitants were sold into slavery. The Cana of the Marriage of John 2 is sought by late tradition at Kufr Kenna, but the town that lay there was called Kanna. "Cana in Galilee" is by that description distinguished from the Tyrian Cana, or Kanah, which lay near Yotapata. The map shows the roads Jesus may have taken from Nazareth to Capernaum.

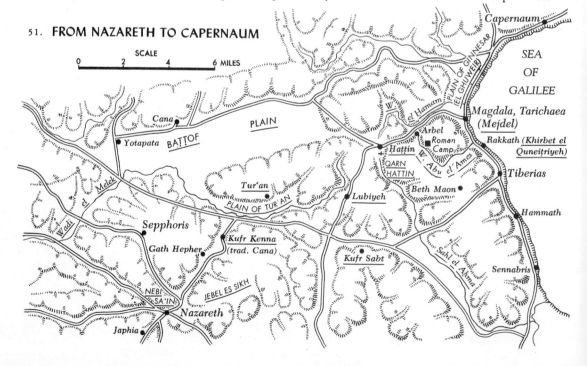

51. FROM NAZARETH TO CAPERNAUM

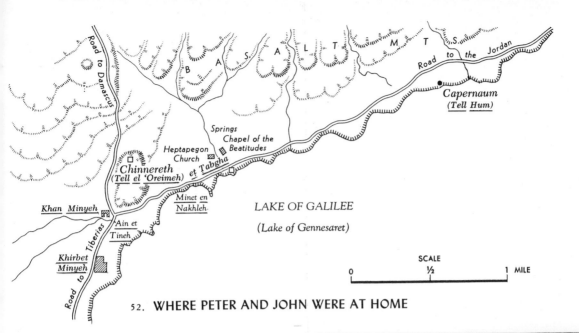

52. **WHERE PETER AND JOHN WERE AT HOME**

52. Capernaum lay near the head of the Lake of Galilee. The great fishing place of the area is at eṭ Ṭabgha, a name derived from the Heptapegon ("Seven Springs") Church that once stood there. Hereabouts one must seek the scene of Mark 1:16f. The tradition that the Sermon on the Mount (Matt. 5:1f.) was held on the hillside above eṭ Ṭabgha is reasonable. This is indeed, the area where a number of incidents of·the Gospels must be localized.

53. The tetrarch Herod Antipas, a son of Herod the Great, governed Galilee and Peraea. He arrested John the Baptist, who thus must have lived in Peraea. Jesus thereupon began his ministry (Mark 1:14). This is a view of Tiberias, on the Lake of Galilee, built by Herod Antipas as his capital and named in honor of the Emperor Tiberius. Much of

54.   KEREN HAYESOD

53.

the ancient city lay in the vacant area. It became an important center of Jewish learning around A.D. 200, when the Mishnah (the basic part of the Talmud) was recorded here. In the 6th-7th centuries the Massoretic "vocalization" of the Hebrew Bible was also developed here. The baths of Tiberias were famous and probably influenced Antipas' choice of site. They lay behind the buildings shown here, the nearest of which is the tomb of Rabbi Meir, a Mishnaic authority of A.D. 130-160.

54. When Jesus came to Capernaum, he attended a synagogue service (Mark 1:21). The synagogue probably stood on the same site where Jews of the 3rd century A.D. built a new synagogue of white limestone. The photo shows the partially restored building. The ruins of the town lie in the narrow plain, bordered by the hillside, up which Jesus must have gone to pray (Mark 1:35). This area is hallowed by memories of him.

71

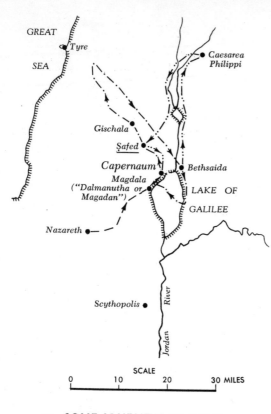

55. SOME JOURNEYS OF JESUS
(According to Mark)

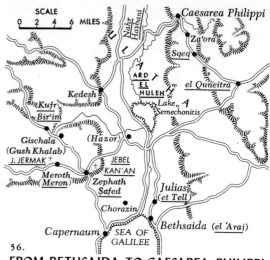

FROM BETHSAIDA TO CAESAREA PHILIPPI

which one of the branches of the Jordan emerges, and called it Caesarea Philippi. On the road to that place occurred the memorable Messianic Confession of Peter (Mark 8:27f.).

57. John's Gospel suggests (*1*) a journey from Nazareth to the place of Baptism and a return going on to Cana (1:29, 43; 2:1f.); then a departure from Nazareth to Capernaum (2:12). (2) A journey from Capernaum to Jerusalem for the Passover (2:

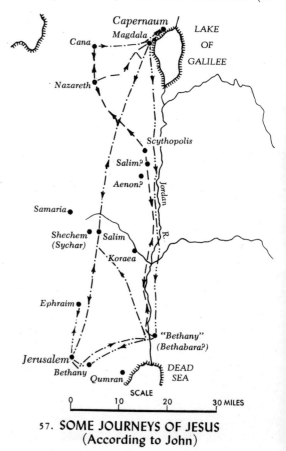

57. SOME JOURNEYS OF JESUS
(According to John)

55. A few journeys of Jesus are traceable in a general way. In Mark 1:16f. we find him going toward Capernaum, and assume he came from Nazareth, for Luke 4:16-30 gives good reason for the emigration. The next journey with any clarity is from Capernaum (7:17) to the territory of Tyre (7:24). Jesus would have been in Tyrian territory soon after leaving Gischala. He then goes back to the Lake of Galilee and the Decapolis (*see* Color Map XVI). An east-west lake crossing to "Dalmanutha" (8:10, but Matt. 15:39 Magadan, for Magdala) follows. The next discernible journey is from Bethsaida (8:22) to Caesarea Philippi (8:27) and then to the "very high mountain" of the Transfiguration (Jebel Jermak near Safed, or even Mt. Hermon?) (9:2). Mt. Tabor, favored by tradition, seems excluded because it bore a pagan sanctuary on its summit. Jesus returned to Capernaum after further Galilean wanderings (9:30, 33).

56. The Gospels speak of Bethsaida, which according to its name was a fishing village. Josephus states that the Tetrarch Philip created a city here and called it Julias after the daughter of Augustus Caesar. It is believed to have lain a short distance inland from the village at a mound called et Tell, but this has never been explored. Philip also rebuilt the Hellenistic city of Paneas at the Pan-grotto, from

13). On the way home he comes into the Judaean country (after a Peraean detour?) and lingers to baptize, not far from John, who is baptizing at Aenon near Salim (3:22-23). Whether the latter is the one near Shechem, or near Scythopolis, is uncertain. (The northern boundary of Judaea was at Koraea.) Jesus then continues to Sychar (Shechem), 4:1f., and thence again goes (via Nazareth?) to Cana in Galilee (4:43, 46). [The Jerusalem journey of 5:1, the lake region travels of 6:1f. and the Gali-

lean wanderings of 7:1 are not considered on the map shown.] (3) The journey to the Feast of the Tabernacles (7:10) being his final departure from Galilee, went via the Jordan Valley (cf. Mark 10:1). From Jerusalem he goes back to the other side of the Jordan (10:40), then returns to Bethany for the raising of Lazarus (11:1f.) and goes on to a place of concealment at "Ephraim" (taken to be eṭ Taiyibeh), and then back again to Jerusalem for the Passion (10:54; 12:1).

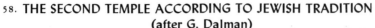

58. THE SECOND TEMPLE ACCORDING TO JEWISH TRADITION
(after G. Dalman)

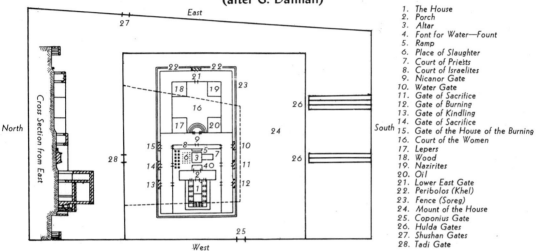

1. The House
2. Porch
3. Altar
4. Font for Water—Fount
5. Ramp
6. Place of Slaughter
7. Court of Priests
8. Court of Israelites
9. Nicanor Gate
10. Water Gate
11. Gate of Sacrifice
12. Gate of Burning
13. Gate of Kindling
14. Gate of Sacrifice
15. Gate of the House of the Burning
16. Court of the Women
17. Lepers
18. Wood
19. Nazirites
20. Oil
21. Lower East Gate
22. Peribolos (Khel)
23. Fence (Soreg)
24. Mount of the House
25. Coponius Gate
26. Hulda Gates
27. Shushan Gates
28. Tadi Gate

58. An Oriental temple was a large enclosure in which at some point there was a "house" of the deity. In front of that was an altar of sacrifice and other appurtenances. In the temple of Herod the "house" is at the bottom of the diagram (at 1) with the Altar east of it (at 3). Worshippers were only permitted to go as far as 8 (the Court of the Israelites). The Court of the Women was at 16, on a

lower level. The "mount of the House" area was lined with colonnades, the one on the east being known as "Solomon's Portico" (Acts 3:11). The Beautiful Gate of Acts 3:10 was the Nicanor Gate (9). The traffic described in Matt. 21:12-13 will have taken place in the porticoes.

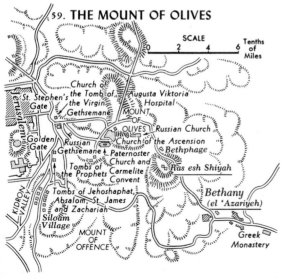

59. THE MOUNT OF OLIVES

59. The Mount of Olives is east of Jerusalem. Bethphage lay to the rear of the summit, according to ancient tradition; it is mentioned in Talmudic sources as the easternmost point in Jerusalem's territory. Bethany was located by tradition at el 'Azariyeh (Lazarus' town). Jesus ascending from Jericho came first to Bethany before going on to Bethphage (Mark 11:1). If there was a city gate corresponding to that of St. Stephen's in Jesus' time he may have entered there. The church of the early centuries located Gethsemane in the area now occupied by the Church of the Tomb of the Virgin Mary. The original Church of the Ascension built for Constantine in 333 stood in the court of the present Carmelite convent. The Mount of Offence gets its name from 2 Kings 23:13. Important tombs are to be seen at the foot of the mount in the Kidron Valley. The Golden Gate was built in the 5th or 6th century A.D., approximately where the East Gate of the Herodian temple stood.

73

The Growth
of Christianity

A DISCIPLE of Jesus named Simon or Peter became the rock on which a Church confessing Jesus as the Christ of God was founded. They called Simon "Cephas" (rock) in recognition of this. He had the first vision of the risen Lord (1 Cor. 15:5). Jesus' brother James also had such a vision (15:7). The last to have one was Saul or Paul of Tarsus (15:8). The Church established itself in Jerusalem. The Christians were Jews living under the Law and worshiping in the temple; their Church was still only a Jewish religious society. "Apostles" or messengers were sent out to win adherents among Jews and Samaritans. But gentiles, too, wanted to become Christians. Paul successfully pleaded for their admission on the basis of confession of faith, without their first becoming Jews. He undertook three great missionary journeys in Asia Minor and Greece c. A.D. 44-57 (Acts 13-20).

A descendant of Herod and Mariamne, named Herod Agrippa, was a friend of Tiberius' successor Caligula (A.D. 37-41). The Roman gave Agrippa the tetrarchy of Philip, and subsequently also that of Agrippa's brother-in-law, Herod Antipas, as well as Abilene in Syria. Claudius (A.D. 41-54) then made Agrippa king also over Judaea and Samaria. Agrippa put James the brother of John to death and imprisoned Peter who, however, escaped and went to Antioch (Acts 12:2, 3, 17; Gal. 2:11). James, the brother of Jesus, now became head of the Church at Jerusalem. Herod Agrippa (I) died in Caesarea in 44.

Procurators were again put in charge of Judaea. Two of them appear in the story of Paul's captivity at Caesarea: Felix (52/3-60) and Festus (60-62). The latter sent Paul to Rome for trial. After Festus' sudden death the Jewish high priest Ananus, as Josephus tells us, had James the brother of Jesus stoned to death. The martyrdom of Peter and Paul probably occurred at Rome in Nero's persecution of A.D. 64.

The design above shows a section of a basilica, with the ground plan of another basilica, as well as two fishes and an anchor from the earliest catacomb paintings—fitting symbols of a new era.

60. AMERICAN GEOGRAPHICAL SOCIETY

60. The city of Samaria was the first city outside of Judaea to hear preaching about Christ (Acts 8:15). Its people with one accord gave heed to Philip's message and there was "great joy in that city." In the 5th century B.C. Samaria had been the seat of the Persian governor of Palestine. With Nehemiah, Judaea became an independent province; with Ezra, fraternization between Jews and Samarians ceased. The latter soon built their own Temple of the Lord at Shechem. Alexander the Great settled Macedonian colonists at Samaria in 331 B.C. It was twice sacked in the Hellenistic era (312 and 296 B.C.); John Hyrcanus besieged it for a year and totally destroyed it (c. 107 B.C.). It was rehabilitated by Pompey's general Gabinius (c. 57-55 B.C.). Augustus gave the city to Herod c. 27 B.C., and through him it was greatly enlarged and beautified in Hellenistic-Roman style. He called it Sebastē (Greek for "Augustus"). One of the noteworthy buildings Herod created was an Augustus-temple. The stairs here shown led up to this temple, but are from the time of Septimius Severus (A.D. 193-211), under whom Sebastē was made a Roman colony.

61. Caesarea was founded by Herod in honor of Caesar Augustus in 22 B.C. and dedicated in 12 B.C. It was a splendid Hellenistic city. The Roman procurators resided here, except for the periods of Archelaus and Herod Agrippa. It had a fine harbor, thanks to Herod's great engineering undertakings. The place was important in early Christian history. The Evangelist Philip lived here (Acts 8:40). Peter visited it (10:24) and Paul was sent to Rome from here after a long detention. Clashes between Jews and gentiles in this place started the Jewish revolt against Rome in A.D. 66. The Crusaders had a city here, but it occupied only a small part of the site. Since their time sand dunes have engulfed Caesarea, but Israeli archaeologists have conducted explorations on the site.

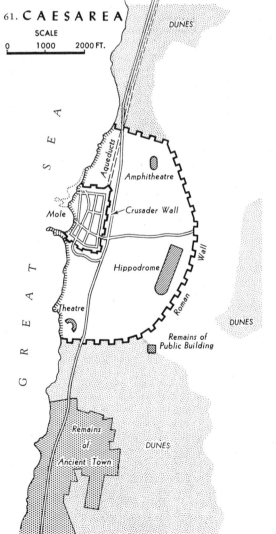

61. CAESAREA

SCALE

0   1000   2000 FT.

75

leucus I Nicator in 300 B.C., it was the capital of his descendants from 240 B.C. until Rome abolished the monarchy in 64 B.C. Coming from Seleucia Pieria, its harbor city, as Paul and Barnabas may have done (Acts 11:26), one crossed the river on a bridge into the old city. South of the main avenue with its colonnades was Epiphaneia, the more modern city-district, named after Antiochus IV Epiphanes. The mighty city walls ascended Mt. Silpius to embrace the acropolis. A clue to the site of the earliest Christian Church may be given by the report that the chair of St. Peter (on which he allegedly was first elevated as bishop) was near the temple of Diana. A terrific earthquake occurred here in A.D. 37 and Roman funds were given to repair the damage. Ultimate decline came in consequence of 5th century earthquakes and the deportation of the inhabitants by Chosroes I in A.D. 538.

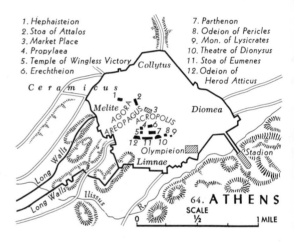

1. Hephaisteion
2. Stoa of Attalos
3. Market Place
4. Propylaea
5. Temple of Wingless Victory
6. Erechtheion
7. Parthenon
8. Odeion of Pericles
9. Mon. of Lysicrates
10. Theatre of Dionysus
11. Stoa of Eumenes
12. Odeion of Herod Atticus

64. ATHENS
SCALE
0   ½   1 MILE

62.   MATSON PHOTO SERVICE

62-63. The coming of Christianity to Antioch (Acts 11:19f.) was an event of great importance, for from here it expanded into the western world. The photo shows Antioch as seen from Mt. Silpius. As the map suggests the acropolis lay behind the point from which the picture was taken. The island in the Orontes River, on which once lay the palaces of mighty kings, is plainly visible. Founded by Se-

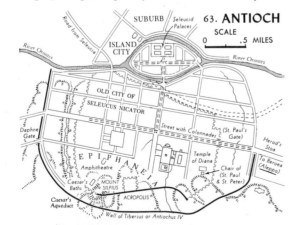

63. ANTIOCH
SCALE
0   .5   MILES

64. Athens is of Biblical-geographical interest because of St. Paul's visit (Acts 17:15f.). Its harbor was Piraeus, and Paul must have arrived there from Thessalonica. In walking to Athens he will have seen altars erected to "unknown gods" as did his contemporary Philostratus. After passing the Ceramicus cemetery, where many of the great men of Athens were buried, he will have entered the city through the Piraeus Gate and come to the market place (agora), a rectangle bordered by many fine public buildings. Recent excavations in this area have identified on its west side ruins of the Stoa or portico of Zeus, the Bouleuterion, in which the Council of the Five Hundred met, etc. From the agora a street leading around the east side of the hill called Areopagus or Mars Hill took one to the main entrance of the Acropolis. Here stood the ornamental gateway called the Propylaea, flanked by the little temple of the Wingless Victory. Passing on one ascended to the Parthenon, beyond which on the northern side of the hilltop was the Erechtheion with its "Porch of the Maidens." But Paul will have avoided all heathen temples.

65. The rocky knoll called Areopagus had been chosen in a bygone age as a fit spot to try crimes. Why the "philosophers" took Paul to the Areopagus (Acts 17:19), rather than to a public forum is puzzling. Did they not wish a larger audience to hear him? No convening of the court is mentioned. One can imagine Paul standing on the rear side of the rock, as shown here, and addressing an audience in the road leading to the Propylaea. Paul's introduction intrigued his sophisticated listeners, but when he began to speak of the coming judgment and the resurrection of Christ, they lost interest. Paul at the Areopagus, facing the shining Parthenon, remains one of the symbolic figures of all time. Here was posed the question how the two heritages can be related—that of Athens and that of Jerusalem, reason and faith, the fulfillment of human personality and the dedication of the person to the eternal.

66. From Athens Paul went to Corinth, where he had more success. No longer the city of classic days, which Romans ravaged in 146 B.C., it had been newly colonized by Julius Caesar. But the ruins of this 6th century B.C. temple of Apollo, with the acropolis hill in the background, still speak of the glory of ancient Corinth. St. Paul's eyes will have rested on it many times in his years at this city, to whose congregation he addressed two great letters which are preserved in the New Testament.

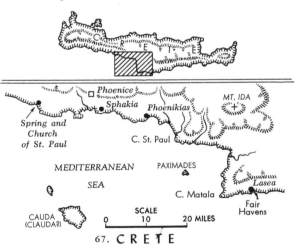

67. **CRETE**

67. On Paul's captivity-journey to Rome he came under the lee of Crete. Coasting along with difficulty they came to Fair Havens, near Lasea. In spite of Paul's warning they tried to reach Phoenix where there was a better harbor. En route a northeaster struck, and they ran under the lee of Cauda. From here they were driven across the sea toward Malta.

77

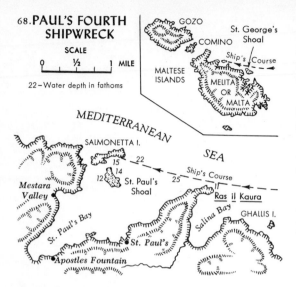

68. PAUL'S FOURTH SHIPWRECK

SCALE

0   ½   1 MILE

22 – Water depth in fathoms

68. Paul reports he was shipwrecked three times (2 Cor. 11:25). So when the vessel struck ground at Malta while making for a beach, it was his fourth shipwreck. A ship coming from the east would have been driven past Ras il Kaura to the western part of St. Paul's Bay. There is a beach here, and south of Salmonetta or Selmun Island a shoal where a vessel could well have grounded. Medieval tradition, however, localized the landing on the eastern part of the bay, where the church of St. Paul *ad mare* was built. In 1610 it was rebuilt and the tower of St. Paul erected. The bay is 8 miles from Valetta and 5 miles from Cita Vecchia, ancient Melite, the capital.

69. Puteoli, now Pozzuoli (*see* Color Map XX-A1), was the landing place of Paul in Italy (Acts 28:13). To get there meant sailing through the Strait of Messina between Italy and Sicily, and going up past Naples and Pompeii. The ruins of the ancient mole of Puteoli, where Paul first stepped on the shores of Italy, are still to be seen. Otherwise, there is not much left of his day except the amphitheater in

which Nero once played an actor's role and the Serapeum. After a stay with Christians Paul went on to Rome. The Appian Way was reached north of Capua. After it left the seashore it went through the Pontine marshes, and the first night's stop was the Forum of Appius, 43 miles from Rome, where friends met him. The next day he reached the end of the marshes at Three Taverns, 33 miles from Rome (near present Cisterna), where a further reception committee met him, to escort him to the eternal city.

70. At Rome the track of Paul ends, for whether he left it alive and was brought back for a second captivity, as legend claims, is uncertain. The Appian Way joined the Ostian Way, coming from the left, near the Circus Maximus. It is by the Ostian Gate that tradition seeks the place of St. Paul's martyrdom. He might have been taken to the Pretorian camp (17), where the centurion Julius would have had to report with his prisoner. Or, if Julius was not of this guard, he might have been taken to the Caelian Hill where the *Princeps Peregrinorum* probably had his headquarters.

The Book of Acts takes no account of Peter's coming to Rome. The tradition that he was imprisoned in the Mamertine Prison (10) and was martyred in the Circus of Gaius and Nero (1) on the mount called *Vaticanus* is very old. The pillar that was put in the square in front of the Church of St. Peter came from that Circus. The belief that Peter was martyred hereabouts led Constantine to build the original Church on this spot, which at the time of the Reformation was replaced by the present structure. Recent excavations under the Church have brought fresh proof that in the 3rd century Peter's resting place was sought here.

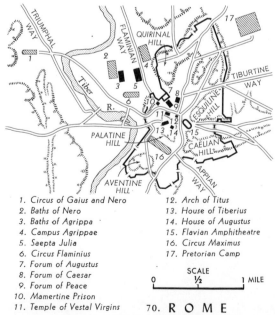

1. Circus of Gaius and Nero
2. Baths of Nero
3. Baths of Agrippa
4. Campus Agrippae
5. Saepta Julia
6. Circus Flaminius
7. Forum of Augustus
8. Forum of Caesar
9. Forum of Peace
10. Mamertine Prison
11. Temple of Vestal Virgins
12. Arch of Titus
13. House of Tiberius
14. House of Augustus
15. Flavian Amphitheatre
16. Circus Maximus
17. Pretorian Camp

SCALE

0   ½   1 MILE

70. ROME

69.   J. LANE MILLER

Table of Early History

CHRONOLOGY	WESTERN ASIA	EGYPT	WESTERN WORLD
3200 B.C.	3200 Early Dynastic Period begins in Babylonia. Erech (Warka) great center.		
3000 B.C.	2900–2600 Jemdet-Nasr Period. Writing begins. 2600 Mesilim, king of Kish. Sumerian Civilization in southern Babylonia.	Before 2850 Kingdoms of North and South, red crown and white crown. 2850 Menes founds first Dynasty. 2850–2190 *Old Kingdom.* Dynasties I-VI. Hieroglyphic writing. 2650 Zoser founds III Dynasty. Pyramid at Sakkara. 2600–2480 IV Dynasty. Cheops, Chephren and Mykerinos. Pyramids at Gizeh.	2600–2000 Early Minoan I-III Periods in Crete. 2600–2200 Early Helladic I-II Periods in Greece. Troy II Period (Schliemann's Treasure of Priam).
2500 B.C.	2500 First Dynasty of Ur. Royal tombs. 2450–2370 Period of the kings of Lagash. 2350 Third Dynasty of Erech. Lugal-zaggisi founds empire. 2350–2150 Dynasty of Akkad (Semites) in northern Babylonia. Prevails over Sumerians. Empire of Sargon I and Naram-Sin. 2150–2050 Dynasty of Gutium, foreign dominion. Fifth Dynasty of Erech. Decline of Palestinian settlements; Amorite invasion? 2050–1950 Third Dynasty of Ur. Kings Ur-Nammu and Shulgi. Last flowering of Sumerian life.	2480–2350 V Dynasty. Sahure, Niuserre; pyramids of Abusir. 2350–2190 VI Dynasty. Pepi I. Campaigns to Sinai and Palestine. Syllabic Script modeled on hieroglyphic writing used at Byblos. 2190–2052 First Intermediate Periods, VII-X Dynasties. 2052–1778 *Middle Kingdom.* Dynasties XI-XII. 2052–1991 XI Dynasty. Mentuhotep of Thebes.	2200–2000 Early Helladic III Period.
2000 B.C.	1975 Amorite ("West Semitic") migration strikes Babylonia. 1950–1698 Dynasties of Isin and Larsa. Lipit-Ishtar of Isin (c. 1870). 1830–1530 First Dynasty of Babylon (West-Semitic or "Amorite"). 1770 Larsa under dominion of Kudur-Mabug of Elam. Warad-Sin king of Larsa. 1758–1698 Rim-Sin, brother and successor of Warad-Sin, conquers Isin. Mari tributary. 1749–1717 Assyrian realm of Shamshi-Adad I. Conquers Mari. Under his son Mari regains independence. Zimri-lim of Mari. References to "Benjaminites." Northern Syria under Khalab (Aleppo) dynasty; Alalakh second seat of king.	1991–1792 XII Dynasty. Amenemhet I-IV; Sesostris I-III. Campaign of Sesostris III to Palestine (c. 1850). 1778–1610 Second Intermediate Period; Dynasties XIII-XVI. 1778–1700 XIII Dynasty; decline of kingdom. 1670–1570 Hyksos period. Dynasties XV-XVI. 1610–715 *New Kingdom;* Dynasties XVII-XXIV. 1610–1570 XVII Dynasty.	2000–1600 Middle Minoan I-III Periods in Crete. Linear A script replaces pictographic writing. 1900–1600 Middle Helladic Civilization in Greece.

Table of Early History, continued

CHRONOLOGY	WESTERN ASIA	EGYPT	WESTERN WORLD
2000 B.C. contd.	1698–1530 Dominance of First Dynasty of Babylon. Mesopotamia and Syria invaded by Hurrians. 1698 Hammurabi, 6th King of Babylon Dynasty, conquers Rim-Sin of Larsa. Destroys Mari. His Law-Code. Founds greatness of Babylon.		
1600 B.C.	1530 Hittites of Asia Minor under Murshilish I overthrow First Dynasty of Babylon. Destroy Khalab in Syria.	1570–1345 XVIII Dynasty. 1570–1545 Amosis, liberator from rule of Hyksos. 1545–1524 Amenophis I. Campaign to Naharina (N.E. Syria and beyond the river). 1524–1502 Thutmosis I and II. 1502–1448 Thutmosis III. 1501–1480 Queen Hatshepsut. Punt Expeditions.	1600–1200 Late Minoan I-III Periods in Crete. 1600–1500 Early Mycenaean Period in Greece.
1500 B.C.	1500–1150 Cassite Dynasty rules at Babylon; 36 Kings. 1500–1200 Ugarit (Ras Shamra) flourishes in Syria. Cuneiform alphabetic script used; elsewhere linear script evolves. 1500 Mitanni Kingdom in Mesopotamia. 1490 Idrimi of Alalakh in Syria and his stela. 1480 Battle of Megiddo. 1460 Telipinush reorganizes Hittite kingdom; his account of Hittite history. 1450 Rise of Hittite Empire. Tudhalia II. Syria becomes part of Hittite orbit.	1480 Thutmosis III. Battle of Megiddo. Conquest of Palestine and Syria. Many campaigns in following decades. 1448–1422 Amenophis II. Asiatic campaigns. 1422–1413 Thutmosis IV. Campaign to Naharina. 1413–1377 Amenophis III. First Amarna letters.	1500–1400 Middle Mycenaean Period. Mycenae, Tiryns, Orchomenos, Pylos.

For those interested in an archaeological dating the following chronology is given.

ARCHAEOLOGICAL CHRONOLOGY

6000–4500 B.C.   NEOLITHIC AGE. (*Men still use stone implements.*)

4500–3200 B.C.   CHALCOLITHIC AGE. (*Some use of copper along with stone.*)

3200–2200 B.C.   EARLY BRONZE AGE.

2200–1550 B.C.   MIDDLE BRONZE AGE.

1550–1200 B.C.   LATE BRONZE AGE.

1200– 330 B.C.   IRON AGE. (*Iron Age I, 1200–900 B.C.; II, 900–650 B.C.; III, 650–330 B.C.*)

Table of Bible History

CHRONOLOGY	HEBREW	WESTERN ASIA	EGYPT	WESTERN WORLD
1400 B.C.	1400 Patriarchal Age in progress (since 1700?). Descent of some Hebrew groups to Egypt.	Amarna Age. Egypt in nominal control of Palestine and Syria. c. 1370 Hittites defeat Mitanni and seize Syria. Assyria independent of Mitanni. 1363–1328 Ashur-uballit I. End of Mitannian Kingdom. 1348 Hittite prince sent to wed widow of Tutankhamen; slain on way. 1345–1315 Murshilish II. Seti I campaign to Palestine. 1315–1290 Muwattalish, Hittite king.	1377–1358 Amenophis IV Akhnaton. 1358–1349 Tutankhamen. 1349–1345 Hui. 1345–1318 XIX Dynasty. 1345–1318 Haremhab. 1318–1317 Ramses I. 1317–1301 Seti I. 1301–1234 Ramses II.	1400 Cretan (Minoan) realm and naval power destroyed. Linear B script: Ionian Greek. 1400–1200 Late Mycenaean Period. 1300 Troy VI destroyed by earthquake.
1300 B.C.	c. 1300 Oppression under Ramses II. c. 1290 Moses born? c. 1230 Exodus of a Hebrew group? c. 1220 "Israel" defeated by Merneptah.	1296 Battle of Kadesh under Ramses II. 1257–1221 Tukulti-Ninurta I of Assyria.	1234–1220 Merneptah reigns; pacifies Palestine; Israel mentioned 1220–1200 Seti II and successors, Siptah Arsu.	
1200 B.C.	c. 1200–1100 Palestine conquered by Hebrews. Tribal confederacy formed.	c. 1197 Sea-peoples migrate on Asiatic coasts, try to invade Egypt. Philistines settle. Tyre refounded by Sidon. 1160 End of Cassite Dynasty at Babylon. 1112–1074 Tiglathpileser I of Assyria. Aramaean migration in Mesopotamia.	1200–1085 XX Dynasty. 1200–1197 Sethnakht. 1197–1165 Ramses III; wards off great invasion of sea-peoples. 1165–1085 Ramses IV–XI.	1200 Beginning of Greek colonization of Aegaean coast of Asia Minor. 1184 Destruction of Troy (VIIa). 1104 Dorian migration.
1100 B.C.	Battle of Taanach. Midianite invasion. c. 1010 Philistine invasion of Central Palestine.	1010–970 Ashur-rabi II of Assyria.	1085–950 XXI Dynasty; Thebes and Tanis, Smendes and Herihor. Wen-Amon's journey to Byblos.	
1000 B.C.	c. 1000–985 Saul. c. 985–963 David. c. 963–929 Solomon. c. 959 Temple completed. c. 929 Secession of northern tribes. **ISRAEL**: c. 929–910 Jeroboam. c. 910–909 Nadab. c. 909–886 Baasha. **JUDAH**: c. 929–913 Rehoboam. c. 913–911 Abijah. c. 911–871 Asa.	969–965 Ashur-resh-ishi II. 964–933 Tiglathpileser II. 932–910 Ashur-dan II. 909–889 Adadnirari II.	950–730 XXII Dynasty (Libyan) 950–929 Shishak (Sheshonk I). Campaign in Palestine. 929–893 Osorkon I.	1000–500 Etruscan Civilization in Italy.
900 B.C.	**ISRAEL**: c. 886–885 Ela. c. 885 Zimri. c. 885–881 Tibni. c. 885–874 Omri. c. 874–851 Ahab. c. 851–850 Ahaziah. c. 850–842 Joram. c. 842–820 Jehu. 842 Jehu submits to Shalmaneser III. c. 820–804 Jehoahaz. c. 804–789 Joash. **JUDAH**: c. 871–850 Jehoshaphat. c. 850–843 Joram. c. 843 Ahaziah. c. 842–836 Athaliah. c. 836–803 Jehoash or Joash. c. 803–775 Amaziah.	888–884 Tukulti-Ninurta II. 883–859 Ashur-nasir-pal II. 858–824 Shalmaneser III. 823–810 Shamshi-Adad V. 809–782 Adad-nirari III.	870–847 Osorkon II. 815–730 Synchronous XXIII Dynasty, King Petubastis and others.	

Table of Bible History, continued

CHRONOLOGY	HEBREW	WESTERN ASIA	EGYPT	WESTERN WORLD
800 B.C.	c. 789–748 Jeroboam II. c. 775–734 Azariah. c. 748 Zechariah. c. 748–734 Jotham regent. c. 748 Shallum. c. 748–736 Menahem. 738 Menahem pays tribute to Tiglathpileser III. c. 736–735 Pekahiah. c. 734–733 Jotham. c. 733–714 Ahaz. c. 714–696 Hezekiah. 701 Hezekiah surrenders to Sennacherib. c. 735–732 Pekah. 733 Tiglathpileser III appoints Hoshea. c. 732–721 Hoshea. 721 Samaria falls.	781–772 Shalmaneser IV. 771–754 Ashur-dan III. 753–746 Ashur-nirari V. 745–727 Tiglathpileser III. 726–722 Shalmaneser V. 721–705 Sargon II. 704–681 Sennacherib. 703 Merodach-baladan II of Babylon.	725 Nubians win control of Egypt; Pi-ankhi. 720–715 XXIV Dynasty: Bocchoris. 715–663 XXV (Nubian) Dynasty. 712–700 Shabaka.	776 Olympic Games begin. c. 770 First Messenian War. 750–550 Second Greek colonization. 753 Traditional date of founding of Rome.
700 B.C.	JUDAH c. 696–642 Manasseh. c. 641–640 Amon. c. 639–609 Josiah. c. 609 Joahaz. 608–598 Jehoiakim.	687 Lydia rises to power in Asia Minor. 680–669 Esarhaddon. 668–648 Shamash-shum-ukin of Babylon. 668–626 Ashurbanipal. 657 Gyges of Lydia dies fighting Cimmerians. 639 End of Elamite kingdom. 625–621 Ashur-etil-ilani. 625–585 Cyaxares of Media. 625–605 Nabopolassar founds Chaldean Dynasty at Babylon. 620–612 Sin-shar-ishkun. 612 Fall of Nineveh. 611–606 Ashur-uballit II. End of Assyria. 605 Battle of Carchemish. Egyptian army crushed. Others defeated at Hamath. 604–562 Nebuchadnezzar II. 604 Nebuchadnezzar interrupts campaign. Visits Babylon to succeed father. Returns to Syria. Sacks Ashkelon in Kislev (Dec.). 601 Nebuchadnezzar tries to invade Egypt. Checkmated in bloody battle.	700–688 Shabataka. 688–663 Tirhaka (Taharka). 670 Egypt conquered by Esarhaddon of Assyria. 667 Ashurbanipal destroys Thebes. 663–525 XXVI Dynasty (Saites). 663–609 Psamtik I. 650 Founding of Naucratis in Egypt. 609–593 Necho.	c. 650 Second Messenian War. 650–580 Corinth powerful in Greece. 650–550 Lydians subdue Greek Asian cities. c. 621 The "Draconic" laws.
600 B.C.	598 (Dec.) Siege of Jerusalem. 598–597 Jehoiachin. 597 Jerusalem surrenders to Nebuchadnezzar 2 Adar (March 16). c. 597–586 Zedekiah. Fall of Jerusalem (August 16, 586). 561 Jehoiachin freed.	599 Operations in Syria and against Arabs. 561–560 Evil-Merodach (Amel-Marduk). 559 Cyrus, Astyages' vassal, begins reign. 555–539 Nabonidus. 550 Cyrus takes over Median realm. 546 Cyrus annexes Croesus' Lydian realm	593–588 Psamtik II. 588–568 Hophra (Apries). 568–525 Amasis. 525 Psamtik III. Cambyses conquers Egypt.	594 Solon lawgiver at Athens. 561–528 Pisistratos dictator at Athens. 510 Fall of Etruscan power; founding of Roman republic.

Date	Greece / Rome	Egypt	Persia and the East	Jews and Palestine
600 B.C. contd.			539 Cyrus takes Babylon. 530 Cambyses reigns; puts aside Smerdis. 525 Cambyses conquers Egypt. Dies 522. Pseudo-Smerdis seizes throne. 521–486 Darius I. Puts down all foes.	
500 B.C.	493–492 **Themistocles, Archon.** Naval program. Fortification of Piraeus, harbor. Miltiades comes to Athens. 490 Darius punishes Greeks. Athenian victory at Marathon. 489 Miltiades dies; Themistocles rules. 480 Persian war of Xerxes. Greeks defeated at Thermopylae; Athens burned. Persian navy defeated at Salamis. 479 Athens again scourged. Battle of Plataea, Pausanias expels Persians. 478–477 **Kimon drives Persians from Thrace.** 431–404 Peloponnesian War. Breaks power of Athens, weakens all Greece.	463 Inaros and Amyrtaeus revolt in Delta. 404 Amyrtaeus (II) rules in Delta. 401 Amyrtaeus sole king of XXVIII Dynasty, rules all Egypt. Persian rule ended.	486–465 Xerxes. 465–424 Artaxerxes I. 424–405 Darius II. 405–359 Artaxerxes II. 401 **Revolt of Cyrus. March of 10,000 Greeks.**	495 Elephantine papyrus attests Jewish colony and temple on island. 458 Ezra's coming? (See 398.) 445 Nehemiah comes to Judea. Rebuilds walls of Jerusalem. 433 Nehemiah returns for a year to Susa. 428 A corrected date for Ezra? 419 Mazzoth festival-order sent to Egyptian Jews by Darius II. 410 Elephantine Jewish temple destroyed. 407 Elephantine Jews' letter to Bagoas, governor of Judaea.
400 B.C.	386 Peace of Antalcidas. Greek cities of Asia Minor recaptured by Persians. 338 Philip defeats Greeks at Chaeronea, establishing Macedonian rule. 338–337 Philip elected Greek Commander of War of revenge against Persia. 336 Philip begins Persian War; murdered. 336–323 Alexander the Great. 335 Alexander destroys rebellious Thebes. 334–331 Conquests of Asia Minor, Syria, Palestine and Egypt. 323–322 Lamian War. Greeks fail to win freedom from Macedonia.	398–393 Nepherites XXIX Dynasty from Mendes in Delta. 358–341 Nektanebos II last of Dynasty XXX from Sebennytos. 343 Artaxerxes III begins Egyptian conquest. 332 Alexander the Great conquers Egypt. 323–306 Ptolemy, satrap of Egypt. 301–31 Ptolemaic Dynasty. 301–285 Ptolemy I Lagi.	359–338 Artaxerxes III. 338–336 Interregnum. Arses. 336–330 Darius III. 333 Battle of Issus won by Alexander the Great. 332 Siege of Tyre. Invasion of Egypt. 331 Battle of Arbela. 330 Alexander burns Persepolis. Ends war of revenge. Dismisses Greek troops. 330–327 Alexander's campaign into Central Asia. 327–325 Alexander's march to India. 324 Marriage festival of Susa. 323 Alexander dies at Babylon. 312 Battle of Gaza; Ptolemy and Seleucus defeat Demetrius. Seleucid era begins. 301 Battle of Ipsus. 301–280 Seleucus I Nicator.	399 End of Elephantine colony. 398 Coming of Ezra to Jerusalem? Founding of Samaritan sect? 348 Rebellion in Syria and Palestine against Artaxerxes III. Jewish groups deported to Hyrcania? 332 Jews come under Macedonian control. 320 Ptolemy I attacks Jerusalem; carries off many captives. 314 Antigonus conquers Palestine. 312 Battle of Gaza gives Ptolemy renewed control.
300 B.C.	264–241 First Punic War. Romans take Sicily. 238 Sardinia and Corsica taken from Carthaginians. 218–201 Second Punic War. 218 Hannibal crosses the Alps. 216 Battle of Cannae. Hannibal wins, but not strong enough to attack Rome. 209 **Scipio takes Carthago Nova in Spain.** 202 Scipio invades Africa. Hannibal defeated. Carthage forced to give up Spain and its navy.	285–246 Ptolemy II Philadelphus. 246–221 Ptolemy III Euergetes. 221–205 Ptolemy IV Philopator. 205–181 Ptolemy V Epiphanes.	280–261 Antiochus I Soter. 261–246 Antiochus II Theos. 261–260 **War between Ptolemy II and Antiochus II.** 246–226 Seleucus II Callinicus. 226–224 Seleucus III Keraunos. 224–187 Antiochus III the Great.	218 Palestine occupied by Antiochus III. 217 **Ptolemy IV retakes Palestine at Raphia.** 202 Palestine retaken by Antiochus III.
200 B.C.	197 Philip V of Macedonia defeated by Romans under Flaminius at Cynoscephalae. 196 Flaminius declares Greeks liberated. 178–168 Perseus, last king of Macedonia. 168 Battle of Pydna; Romans destroy Macedonian kingdom.	181–146 Ptolemy VI Philometor. 164–162 Jewish temple founded at Leontopolis in Egypt by Onias IV, son of high priest Onias III.	187–175 Seleucus IV Philopator. 175–164 Antiochus IV Epiphanes. 174 Antiochus IV visits Jerusalem. 169 First Egyptian campaign of Antiochus. 168 Second Egyptian campaign of Antiochus. 167–166 Appeal of the Samaritans.	200 Palestine lost to Scopas, Ptolemy's general. 198 Palestine definitely becomes Seleucid. Scopas beaten at Paneas and Sidon. 190 **Simon the Maccabee is high priest.** c. 176 Heliodorus seeks to rob Temple for Seleucus IV.

84

CHRONOLOGY	HEBREW	WESTERN ASIA	EGYPT	WESTERN WORLD
200 B.C. contd.	175 Antiochus IV replaces Onias III with Jason as high priest. Hellenization begun at Jerusalem. 172 Jason replaced by Menelaos. 170 Onias III assassinated. 169 Antiochus plunders the Temple. 168 Revolt in Jerusalem. Punitive raid of Apollonius. Theocracy abolished. Greek *Polis* founded in City of David (*Acra*). 167 Temple polluted. Maccabeans revolt. 166-165 Death of Mattathias of Modiin. Book of Daniel. 165 Gorgias proceeds against Maccabees. Campaign of Lysias. 164 Persecution ceases. Temple rededicated (*Hanukkah Festival*). 163 At death of Antiochus IV Judas besieges Acra. Campaign of Antiochus V. 162 Peace made; Temple returned to Jews. Menelaos executed. Alcimus high priest. Demetrius overthrows Antiochus V. 161 Jews rebellious; Judas' victory over Nicanor. Judas' treaty with Rome? 160 Campaign of Bacchides. Judas slain. 160-142 Jonathan. 159 Alcimus dies; no successor appointed. c. 157 Jonathan makes peace with Seleucids. 152 Alexander Balas appoints Jonathan high priest.	166-163 **Antiochus' expedition to the East.** 163 Death of Antiochus in eastern campaign. 163-162 **Antiochus V Eupator.** 162-150 Demetrius I Soter, son of Seleucus IV.		166 Romans make Delos a free harbor; end of importance of Rhodes.
150 B.C.	143 Trypho, commander of Antiochus VI, seizes and executes Jonathan. Simon Maccabeus sides with **Demetrius II.** 142-134 Simon. 142 Demetrius II gives autonomy to Jews. 141 Simon captures the Acra. 140 Simon appointed Ethnarch. 139-138 Antiochus VII grants Jews privileges. 134 Simon assassinated; son of John Hyrcanus made high priest. Antiochus VII takes Jerusalem; confirms autonomy. 134-104 John Hyrcanus. 104-103 Aristobulus. 103-76 Alexander I Jannaeus.	151-145 Alexander Balas, usurper. 146-138 Demetrius II Nicator. 140 Parthian campaign of Demetrius II. Falls into captivity. 138-129 Antiochus VII Sidetes. 133 Attalus of Pergamum wills realm to Rome. It becomes province of Asia. 128-125 Demetrius II Nicator. 128-122 Alexander Zabinas. 125 Seleucus V. 125-113 Antiochus VIII Grypos. 113-95 Antiochus IX Kyzikenos. 111-96 Antiochus VIII.		149-146 Third Punic War. Carthage razed. 148 Macedonian uprising. Macedonia, Epirus and Thessaly made Roman province. 146 War between Sparta and Achaeans. Roman general Mummius destroys Corinth. Greece tributary. 133 The Gracchi begin movement to help the poor.
100 B.C.	76-67 Salome Alexandra. 67-63 Aristobulus II younger son prevails over Hyrcanus II elder son. 63 Romans take Jerusalem Temple. Judaea Roman dependency; Hyrcanus made high priest. Origin of the Decapolis.	93 Tigranes of Armenia takes Cappadocia. 89-88 Mithridates of Pontus conquers Bithynia, **Phrygia and Mysia. Athens** allies itself with Mithridates. 88-85 First Mithridatic War. Sulla. 85 Mithridates forced back into Pontus.	96 Apion, son of Ptolemy VIII, bequeathes Cyrenaica to Rome. 42-31 Antony ruler of East. 37 Antony weds Cleopatra. 32-31 Octavian wars on Cleopatra, de-	92 Contact between Rome and Parthians. Fortifica- 87-86 Sulla besieges Athens. Fortifications razed, Piraeus burned. 63 Conspiracy of Catiline. 58-51 Caesar's Gallic Wars.

(Table continued from left)

CHRONOLOGY	HEBREW	ROME
100 B.C. contd.	63-40 Hyrcanus II. Antipater governor of Judaea. 47 Hyrcanus hereditary high priest and ethnarch of the Jews. 46 Antipater's sons Phasael and Herod commanders of Judaea and Galilee. 44 At death of Caesar, Antipater and Herod support Cassius. 43 Antipater assassinated. 41 Phasael and Herod tetrarchs. 40 Parthian invasion; Hasmonaean Antigonus made king; Rome offers kingship to Herod, if he can win it. 38 Herod defeats Antigonus' commander at Isana. 37 Herod captures Jerusalem. Antigonus executed at Antioch. 20 Herod receives from Augustus the Hauran and Batanaea; also Ituraean Tetrarchy of Zenodorus. 20-19 Begins rebuilding of Temple. 10 Temple completed. 7 Alexander and Aristobulus executed. 6-4 Varus, legate of Syria. 4 Herod's son Antipater executed. Herod dies. Uprising suppressed by Varus. 4-6 A.D. Archelaus Ethnarch of Judaea, Idumaea and Samaria. 4-34 A.D. Philip Tetrarch of Batanaea, Trachonitis, Auranitis and "Ituraea." 4-37 A.D. Lysanias Tetrarch of Abilene in Syria. 4-39 A.D. Herod Antipas Tetrarch of Galilee and Peraea.	83 Tigranes conquers Seleucid realm. 83-81 Second Mithridatic War. 69 Tigranes defeated at Tigranocerta by Lucullus. Disaster in Parthian campaign. 68-64 Antiochus XIII, last Seleucid king. 54-53 Crassus, legate of Syria. Invades Mesopotamia, is defeated by Parthians at Haran (Carrhae). 52 Pompey sole Consul. 49 Break between Caesar and Pompey. Caesar gets control of Italy and Spain. Pompey goes to Greece. 48 Battle of Pharsalus. Pompey defeated by Caesar; flees to Egypt and is slain. 48-47 Alexandrian War. Caesar intervenes in Egypt. 47 End of Kingdom of Pontus through Caesar's defeat of Pharnaces. 39 Antony defeated in Parthian venture. 44 Caesar slain. Antony rules Rome. Opposed by Octavian and Consuls. 43 Triumvirate of Antony, Octavian, and Lepidus. 42 Battle of Philippi. Death of Brutus and Cassius. 36 Lepidus retires. Octavian ruler of West. 33 Break between Antony and Octavian. 31 Battle of Actium. 30 Death of Antony and Cleopatra. Octavian rules Roman realm. 27 Octavian becomes Augustus Caesar.
I A.D.	6 Second term of Quirinius. Census of Palestine. Uprising of Judas "the Galilaean." Procurators rule Judaea. 27-37 Pilate, procurator. c. 30 Death of Jesus. 34 Tetrarchy of Philip abolished. c. 35 Paul's conversion? 37 Herod Agrippa I given tetrarchy of Philip and that of Abilene. 38-39 Anti-Jewish rioting in Alexandria. 40 Agrippa gets Tetrarchy of Antipas. 41-44 Herod Agrippa I made king and rules realm of Herod the Great by favor of Claudius. 41-48 Herod of Chalcis, husband of Berenice. 44 Dispersal of the Apostles. James the Just at helm of Jerusalem Church. 44-48 Procuratorial government for Judaea under Cuspius Fadus and Tiberius Alexander. 48-52 Ventidius Cumanus procurator. 49 Claudius expels Jews from Rome. 50 Herod Agrippa II gets kingdom of Chalcis. 52-60 Antonius Felix procurator. 53 Agrippa II gives up Chalcis but receives old tetrarchies of Philip and Lysanias. 57 Paul goes to Jerusalem. 58-60 Paul prisoner in Caesarea. 60-62 Porcius Festus procurator. 64 Persecution of Nero. 64-66 Gessius Florus procurator. 66 Cestius Gallus gives up siege of Jerusalem. 66-73 Jewish War. 67 Vespasian subjects Galilee and Samaria. 68 Peraea and Idumaea pacified. 70 Titus begins siege of Jerusalem. City falls in September. 73 Fall of Masada. Jewish uprisings in Alexandria and Cyrene.	14 Death of Augustus. 14-37 Tiberius. 37-41 Caius Caligula. 41-54 Claudius. 54-68 Nero. 68-69 Galba. Otho. Vitellius. 69-79 Vespasian. 79-81 Titus. 81-96 Domitian. 96-98 Nerva. 98-117 Trajan (co-regent in 97).
100 A.D.	100 Death of Agrippa II. His kingdom made part of Syrian province. 106 Nabataean kingdom becomes province of Arabia. 116-117 Jewish uprisings in Alexandria, Cyrene, Cyprus, Mesopotamia, Palestine. 132-135 Uprising of Barcochba. Beth-Ter last resistance. Aelia Capitolina founded on site of Jerusalem.	117-138 Hadrian.

(continued at right)

Index to Color Maps

This index refers to the color maps found on pages 9-48. Each map name has an index reference key, always a letter and figure combination, and the plate numbers of the maps in roman numerals.

Paraetonium ....C2 XIII
Paran ....C6 V
Paropamisus (Hindukush) ..
C13 XIII
Parthia (Parthava) .C10 XII;
C7 XIII
Pasargadae.C7 III; D9 XII;
C7 XXI
Patara..............B4 XX
Pathros.............D3 XI
Patmos, isl.........B4 XX
Patrae..D10 XIX; B3 XX
Pattala............E12 XII
Pekod................C6 XII
Pella A1 XIII; D4 XIV, XV,
XVI; C10 XIX; A3 XX
Pelusium.D5 XII; C3 XIII;
E12 XIX; C5 XX
Penuel...D4 VI, VII, VIII,
IX, X
Peraea......E4 XV, XVI
Perga...............B5 XX
Pergamum...B2 XI, XIII,
XXI; C4 XII; D11 XIX;
B4 XX
Perinthus..........A4 XX
Persepolis ....D7 XIII;
E9 XII; C7 XXI
Persis (Parsa).....E9 XII;
D7 XIII
Pessinus............B5 XX
Petra.......C4 XIII, XXI;
E13 XIX; C6 XX
Pharpar, riv....B5 VI, VII,
VIII, IX, X, XIV, XV, XVI
Pharsalus...........B3 XX
Phasaelis.D3 XIV, XV, XVI
Phiala (Birket Ran), lake...
A3 II
Philadelphia (in Asia Minor)
B4 XX
Philadelphia (Rabbath Am-
mon)...C4 XIII; E4 XIV,
XV, XVI
Philippi......A1 XIII; C10
XIX; A3 XX
Philoteria (Beth Yerah)....
C4 XIV, XV, XVI
Phoenicia....A2 I; B3 XIV,
XV, XVI; C6 XX
Phoenix ....B3 XX
Phrygia..C4 XII; D11 XIX
Pirathon..D3 VI, VII, VIII,
IX, X
Pisidia....C5 XII; B3 XIII;
D12 XIX
Pithom, Heroonpolis (Tell
Ertabeh)....B3 V; C3 III
Podandus...........B6 XX
Pompeii.............A1 XX
Pontus....A3 XI; A4 XIII;
C13 XIX
Priene.....B4 XX; B2 XXI
Prymnessus.........B4 XX
Pteria..............A5 XX
Ptolemais (Acco)...C3 XIII,
XIV, XV, XVI; C6 XX
Ptolemais (in Egypt).......
D3 XIII; E10 XIX
Punon ....B7 V
Put ....B5 IV
Puteoli ....A1 XX
Pydna...............A3 XX

QATNA.............C4 III
Que ....B4 XI
Qumran, Khirbet...E4 XIV,
XV; E2 XXI

RAAMSES?.........B3 V
Rabbath Ammon (Phila-
delphia; Amman)...C3 II;
E5 VI, VII, VIII, IX, X;
E4 XIV, XV, XVI
Rabbath Moab..F4 VI, VII,
VIII, IX, X
Raga................C9 XIII
Ragaba..D4 XIV, XV, XVI
Rakkath..C3 VI, VII, VIII,
IX, X
Ram, mtn.....E3 II; C7 V;
D4 XII
Ramah (NW of Galilee)....
C3 VI, VII, VIII, IX, X
Ramah (Ramathaim).E3 VI,
VII, VIII, IX, X, XIV,
XV, XVI
Ramoth (Gilead).....C5 VI,
VII, VIII, IX, X
Raphana.C5 XIV, XV, XVI
Raphia..E2 III; A6 V; C3
XI, XIII; F1 XIV, XV,
XVI; C5 XX
Raṣappa ....B5 XI

Ras esh Shamra.....B4 XI;
B3 XXI
Rehob..E2 III; D4 VI, VII,
VIII, IX, X
Rehoboth.....A6 V; F2 VI,
VII, VIII, IX, X
Rekem (Petra).B7 V; C4 XI
Remeth..C4 VI, VII, VIII,
IX, X
Rephaim, Plain of......C2 I
Rephidim............D5 V
Retenu...............C3 III
Rezeph (Raṣappa)....B4 XI
Rhagae..............B7 III
Rhinocorura ....C3 XIII
Rhodes (Rhodus)...C4 XII;
B2 XIII; D11 XIX; B4 XX
Riblah...............C4 XI
Rimmon (Ephraim)..E3 VI,
VII, VIII, IX, X
Rimmon (Galilee)...C3 VI,
VII, VIII, IX, X
Rithmah.............C7 V
Rome (Roma).....C8 XIX;
A1 XX
Rosetta ....A2 V

SABTA ....D6 IV
Sabteca ....D6 IV
Safed.B4 XIV; C4 XV, XVI
Sais...........C3 XI; D5 XII;
C5 XX
Salamis...C5 XII; B3 XIII;
D12 XIX; B5 XX
Salecah..D6 XIV, XV, XVI
Salim....D4 XIV, XV, XVI
Sam'al ....B4 XI
Samaria, reg..B2 I; D3 VI,
VII, VIII, IX, X, XIV,
XV, XVI; C4 XI; C3 XIII;
C5 XV, XVI, XX
Samaria (Sebaste).D3 XIV,
XV, XVI; C6 XX
Samosata......B4 XI, XIII;
C6 XII
Samothrace, isl......A4 XX
San'a ....D6 IV
Sardinia, isl........D7 XIX
Saqqara ....C3 V
Sardis....B2 III, XI, XIII,
XXI; D1 IV; C4 XII;
D11 XIX; B4 XX
Sarepta..B3 XIV, XV, XVI
Sarmatia..........A10 XIX
Schedia ....C5 XX
Scythopolis C3 XIV, XV, XVI
Seba...............D5 IV
Sebastiyeh ....D2 XXI
Sebennytos.........B3 V
Seir, mount...C3 II; B7 V
Seleucia..B3 XIII; C4 XIV,
XV, XVI; E14 XIX; B5 XX
Seleucia (in Babylonia).....
C5 XIII
Seleucia Pieria....B4 XIII;
B6 XX
Seleucis............B4 XIII
Selinus...D12 XIX; B5 XX
Semechonitis, lake....A2 I;
A3 II; B4 VI, VII, VIII,
IX, X, XV, XVI; B3 XIV
Sepharad (Sardis)...C4 XII
Sepphoris C3 XIV, XV, XVI
Serabiṭ el Khadem....D5 V;
D3 XI
Sewen (Syene, Assuan)....
E3 XI
Shamiramalti........B5 III
Shankhar...........B5 III
Sharon, Plain of..B1 I; B2
II; D2 VI, VII, VIII, IX,
X, XIV, XV, XVI
Sharuhen....E2 III; F1 VI,
VII, VIII, IX, X
Sheba ....D6 IV
Shechem (Sychar).B2 I; C4,
E2 III; D3 VI, VII, VIII,
IX, X, XIV, XV, XVI
Shephelah ....C1 I
Shiloh...D3 VI, VII, VIII,
IX, X
Shimron..C3 VI, VII, VIII,
IX, X
Shimron-meron..B3 VI, VII,
VIII, IX, X
Shinar: see Babylonia
Shuah..............C5 XI
Shunem.E2 III; C3 VI, VII,
VIII, IX, X, XIV, XV, XVI
Shupria............B5 XI
Shur, Wilderness of...B5 V
Shushan-Susa (Shush).....
C6 XI, XXI
Side......B3 XIII; B5 XX

Sidon.A2 I; A3 II, VI, VII,
VIII, IX, X, XIV; C4 III,
XI, XIII, XV, XVI; D5
XII; E13 XIX; C6 XX
Sile................B4 V
Simeon.............F2 VI
Simonias.C3 XIV, XV, XVI
Sin, Wilderness of.....B5 V
Sinai (Jebel Musa), mtn...
D6 V; D3 XI
Sinope......D2 IV; A4 XI,
XIII; B6 XII; C13 XIX;
A6 XX
Sin-Pelusium..A4 V; C3 XI
Sippar...........C5 III, XI
Sipylus, mtn....B2 III, XI;
B4 XX
Sirbonis, lake........A5 V
Smyrna...B2 III, XI, XIII;
D11 XIX; B4 XX
Socoh....E2 VI, VII, VIII,
IX, X
Socotra.............D7 IV
Sogdiana ....C12 XII
Soli.......B3 XIII; B5 XX
Strymon............A3 XX
Subartu............B5 III
Succoth (Scenae)....D4 VI,
VII, VIII, IX, X, XIV,
XV, XVI
Sukhu (Shuah).......C5 XI
Sumer..............C6 III
Susa (Shushan)....C6 III,
XIII; D8 XII
Susiana.............D8 XII
Sutu................C4 III
Syene....F5 XII; E3 XIII;
G12 XIX
Sykaminos C2 XIV, XV, XVI
Synnada...........B5 XX
Syracusae..D9 XIX; B2 XX
Syrian Gates........B6 XX
Syrtis Major......E9 XIX;
C2 XX
Syrtis Minor ....E8 XIX

TAANACH....C3 VI, VII,
VIII, IX, X
Taanath-shiloh..D3 VI, VII,
VIII, IX, X
Tabali.............B4 XI
Tabor, mtn: see Itabyrion...
B2 I; B3 II; C3 VI, VII,
VIII, IX, X, XIV, XV,
XVI
Tacapae...........E7 XIX
Tadmor (Palmyra)..C4 III,
XI, XIII; D6 XII
Tahpanhes (Daphnae).B3 V;
C3 XI
Takritain..........C5 XI
Tanis.........C2 III; B3 V
Tappuah..D3 VI, VII, VIII,
IX, X
Tarentum.B2 XII; C9 XIX;
A2 XX
Tarichaea.C3 XIV, XV, XVI
Tarshish (Tartessus)....A2,
B1 IV
Tarsus....C5 XII; B4 XIII,
XXI; D13 XIX; B5 XX
Taurus, mts....B3 III; B4,
B6 XX
Tavium.............B5 XX
Taxila............D13 XII
Tekoa...E3 VI, VII, VIII,
IX, X, XIV, XV, XVI
Telmissus.........B2 XIII
Tema...........D4 XI, XIII
Teman...............B7 V
Thamar..B7 V; G3 VI, VII,
VIII, IX, X
Thamna..D3 XIV, XV, XVI
Thapsacus.C6 XII; B4 XIII
Thasos............A3 XX
Thebes (Thebae, No Amon).
B3 III, XI; D1 IV; E3 V;
E5 XII; D3 XIII; F12 XIX
Thebes (in Greece)..B3 XX
Thebez...D3 VI, VII, VIII,
IX, X
Theku...............B3 V
Thessalonica (Thessalonice).
A1 XIII; C10 XIX;
A3 XX
Thmuis.............A3 V
Thrace (Thracia), reg.......
C2 IV; A2 XIII; C11
XIX; A4 XX
Thracians (Skudra).B3 XII
Three Taverns......A1 XX
Thyatira...........B4 XX
Tiberias..C3 XIV, XV, XVI
Til Barsip.........B4 III

Timnah..E2 VI, VII, VIII,
IX, X
Timnath-serah..D3 VI, VII,
VIII, IX, X
Tiphsah (Thapsacus)..B4 XI
Tirqa........C5 III; B5 XI
Tiryns.............B1 III
Tirzah...D3 VI, VII, VIII,
IX, X
Tmolus, mtn........B2 XI
Tobiah, House of...D4 XIV
Togarmah..........B5 IV
Tophel.............B7 V
Trachonitis ......B5 XIV,
XV, XVI
Tralles ....B4 XX
Trapezus (Trebizond)....A4
XI, XIII; B6 XII; C14 XIX
Tripolis....C4 XIII; C6 XX
Troas.............B4 XX
Troy...............B2 III
Tubal..............B5 IV
Tumilat, Wadi......C3 III
Tunip..............C4 III
Tuspa..............B5 XI
Tyana..B3 XIII; D12 XIX;
B5 XX
Tyre: see also Tyrus..A2 I;
A3 II; C4, D2 III; D2 IV;
B3 VI, VII, VIII, IX, X,
XIV; D6 XII; C3 XI,
XIII; C5 XV, XVI, XX
Tyrian Ladder.A2 I; B3 VI,
VII, VIII, IX, X, XIV,
XV, XVI
Tyrus....C4 XIII; E4 XIV,
XV, XVI; E13 XIX

UGARIT (Ras esh Shamra).
B4 III
Ulai, riv............C6 XI
Ulatha...B4 XIV, XV, XVI
Umma...............C6 III
Upi................C4 III
Ur........C6 III, XI
Urartu.............B5 XI
Urhai (Edessa)......C6 XII
Uz.................B5 IV
Uzal ....D6 IV

VERONA...........B8 XIX
Vesuvius, mtn.......A1 XX

WARKA...........C6 XXI
Wassukanni.........B3 III
Wilderness of Shur....B5 V
Wilderness of Sin.....B5 V
Wilderness of the
Wandering.........C5 V
Wilderness of Zin....B7 V;
G3 VI, VII, VIII, IX, X

XANTHUS.....C4 XII; B2
XIII

YADNANA (Cyprus), isl...
C3 XI
Yamkhad...........B4 III
Yamuthal..........C6 III
Yarmuk, riv..B3 II; C4 VI,
VII, VIII, IX, X, XIV,
XV, XVI
Yeb (Elephantine Isl.).....
E3 XI
Yehud..............D6 XII
Yenoam.....C4 VI, VII,
VIII, IX, X
Yotapata (Jodephath).......
C3 XIV, XV, XVI

ZADRAKARTA....B7 XIII
Zanoah..F2 VI, VII, VIII,
IX, X
Zaphon (Asaphon)...D4 VI,
VII, VIII, IX, X, XIV,
XV, XVI
Zaphon (Casius), mtn.B4 III
Zarephath......B3 VI, VII,
VIII, IX, X; C3 XI
Zarethan..D4 VI, VII, VIII,
IX, X
Zered, riv.....A7 V; G4 VI,
VII, VIII, IX, X
Zeugma...........B4 XIII
Ziklag....F2 VI, VII, VIII,
IX, X
Ziph: see Wilderness of
Ziph F3 VI, VII, VIII. IX, X
Zoan...............C3 XI
Zoar (Zoara)...F4 VI, VII,
VIII, IX, X, XIV, XV, XVI
Zobah (Aram-zobah)..C4 XI
Zorah.........E2 III, VI,
VII, VIII, IX, X

88